MW01641326

Enjoy!
Good Friends
Good Food
[illegible]

Life Beyond Takeout!

Paula Guiliano

Paul Ropski

Jim Karagianes

Fran Karagianes

Bill Gorgo

Geneva Gorgo

Marilyn Aleide

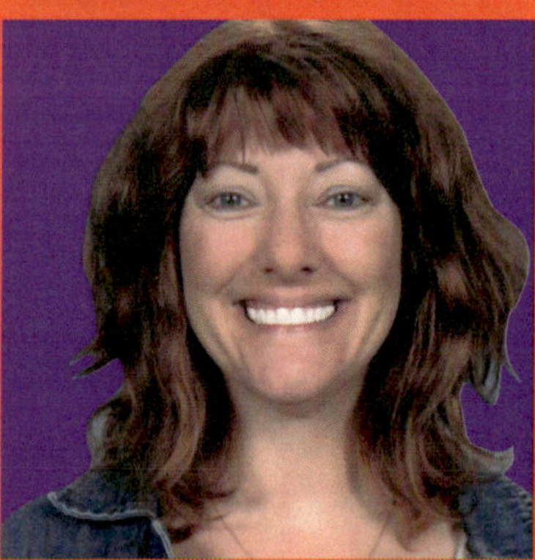
Julie DeMicco

Life Beyond Takeout!

Chicago's fabulous foodies speak out about food, wine & life.

BY PAULA GUILIANO

CO-AUTHORS:
PAUL ROPSKI
JIM KARAGIANES
FRAN KARAGIANES
BILL GORGO
GENEVA GORGO
MARILYN ALEIDE

EDITED BY JULIE DEMICCO

SPECIAL FEATURE: WINE & BEER
MANFRED BAUER, OWNER/CEO,
WEIN-BAUER, INC.

Surround yourself with the people
you love and share your most intimate
and funny stories, while breaking bread
together... and taste life in many new ways.

Library of Congress 2011932830

ISBN 978-0-7414-6744-7 Hard Cover

ISBN 978-0-7414-6745-4 Soft Cover

ISBN 978-0-7414-7547-3 eBook

INFINITY PUBLISHING
1094 New DeHaven Street, Suite 100
West Conshohocken, PA 19428-2713
Toll-free (877) BUY BOOK
Local Phone (610) 941-9999
Fax (610) 941-9959
Info@buybooksontheweb.com
www.buybooksontheweb.com
www.lifebeyondtakeout.com

First Edition.
Printed in the United States of America.

CONCEPT & DESIGN

Paula Guiliano

PHOTOGRAPHY

Paula Guiliano

Paul Ropski

Bill Gorgo

Geneva Gorgo

PRODUCTION

Sarah Koz

Dedication

I dedicate this book to my dear friend Paul Ropski who inspired me to take on this culinary project for the preservation of our beloved family and original recipes.

Paul helped to breathe life into a stagnant project, he encouraged me to always buy local, can fresh and to celebrate the art of culinary shopping at its best through Green City Markets and gourmet shops in search of the perfect ingredients and new ideas.

To my co-authors, Jim Karagianes and Fran Karagianes, Bill Gorgo and Geneva Gorgo, and Marilyn Carinci Aleide who embraced this project with love, and who generously gave of their time, talent and recipes, which helped make this cookbook possible. This includes all of the noteworthy relatives and friends who provided recipes, guidance or inspiration over the years, which significantly influenced this collection and our life stories in so many ways.

To my mother, Josephine (Pacelli) Guiliano, and my grandmother Pasqalina Guiliano who taught me the essentials of authentic regional Napolitano style cooking as a means to bringing family and friends together as it defined a way of life for three generations.

To Sandra Weiss, who for the past twenty years has embraced every one of my endeavors with enthusiasm, allowing me to shine and to reach for the stars.

Acknowledgements

A special thanks to Manfred Bauer, Tobias Lehmen and Kimberly Goodwin from Wein-Bauer, Inc for their support, time and talent in providing the research, pairing notes, logos, labels and photographs for the special feature on Wine & Beer. This feature elevated Life Beyond Takeout! to a new level. The Wein-Bauer Team supported this project with grace and compassion and gave of their time willingly in order to provide the right blending of the recipes with superb pairing options. Without their support this part of the book would not be possible.

Tobias Lehmen
Regional Sales Manager/
German Wine Expert
Wein-Bauer, Inc

Manfred Bauer
Owner/CEO
Wein-Bauer, Inc

Kimberly Goodwin
Regional Sales Manager/
Marketing & Communications
Wein-Bauer, Inc

Introduction

Life Beyond Takeout! takes you on an engaging culinary journey into the art of good cooking made easy through time-tested family and original recipes. Dine in with us and explore comfort foods and signature dishes from seven of Chicago's self-professed fabulous foodies who have perfected the art of transforming the ordinary into the delectable.

For those of us who cherish time-honored traditions of cooking and baking, and the true joy of sharing with those we love, we have included 85 recipes, carefully chosen and beautifully presented to cover just about every occasion; from intimate city dinners, to grand celebrations. These recipes are simple and satisfying, elegant and elaborate, comforting and homey; all ideal for the occasional chef or seasoned expert.

Consider this experience a "food frenzy" with a touch of modern sensibilities that will help you learn the art of cooking gourmet, or if you desire, the act of improvising so you can feel comfortable moving away from a set of defined ingredients with a sense of freedom and imagination to create your own dish from our recipe collection.

Our hope is to open up a sophisticated world of tastes and smells for you to discover. We are a passionate group of foodies who like to eat, and we have perfected the art of *good eating* by combining fresh ingredients with easy to follow recipes that taste great. This colorful collection of good smells and great tastes is meant to tease your senses and stimulate your imagination.

Explore intimate conversations about family from a group of inspired chefs who have generously contributed their recipes to create this marvelous collection of regional European and American cuisine with Italian, Greek, Polish and Jewish influences.

Enjoy a special feature on wine and beer pairing brought to you by Wein-Bauer, Inc., a world renowned importer of wine, spirits and beer. The Wein-Bauer Team, has taken the guess work out of the pairing process, while providing a refresher on wine and beer education. You'll also find an amazing list of medal winners and in-depth company profiles from Austria, Germany and Italy so you can experience the family tradition and passion behind some of their recommendations.

Paula Guiliano

Paula Guiliano

ORGANICALLY GROWN

Fresh Content

Rec-i-pes (noun): A series of step-by-step instructions for preparing ingredients you forgot to buy, with utensils you don't own, only to make a dish the dog won't eat.

Paula Guiliano

1

Appetizers

Asparagus Frittata

PREP TIME: 15 MINUTES **COOK TIME: 25 MINUTES** **TOTAL: 40 MINUTES** **SERVES 2–4**

INGREDIENTS

1	pound asparagus spears
8	large eggs
½	cup milk
8	oz. shredded Mozzarella
2	tbsps. grated Romano cheese
1	tbsp. olive oil
½	tsp. salt
1	tsp. black pepper

Just about any cooked vegetable will work in this recipe—I've made it with leftover pasta—but asparagus is my family's all-time favorite.

PREPARATION

- Trim the asparagus and steam or roast until tender. Cut into 1-inch pieces and set aside.
- Beat eggs and milk together.
- Preheat broiler. Heat an ovenproof pan—preferably well-seasoned cast iron—over medium heat. Add olive oil and heat for a minute or two. Add egg mixture.
- After 2 minutes, add the asparagus pieces, then the cheese, salt, and pepper. Continue to cook, using a butter knife or thin spatula to separate the cooked eggs from the sides of the pan while tipping the pan so that uncooked eggs from the top run into the ditch you've created.
- When the eggs have set sufficiently so that nothing runs when you tip the pan, pop it under the broiler for 90 seconds. Place a serving plate on top of pan and flip out the frittata.

Wine Pairing

A fresh and lively white wine with citrusy and slight floral aromas and balanced acidity such as a Sauvignon Blanc.

SUGGESTION: Aromo Varietal Sauvignon Blanc.

Crab and Shrimp Croissants

PREP TIME: 15 MINUTES COOK TIME: 20 MINUTES TOTAL: 35 MINUTES SERVES 4–6

INGREDIENTS

1	prepackaged croissant rolls
4	oz. tub whipped cream cheese
4	oz. can small deveined shrimp
4	oz. can white crab meat
½	cup powdered sugar
¼	cup shrimp sauce
¼	cup ketchup

This is a tasteful dish for shell-fish "lovers" served in a beautiful presentation. The combination of the shrimp and crab flavors are offset by the sweet taste of the flaky croissant with an added powdered sugar sprinkle.

PREPARATION

- Prepare packaged croissants in the oven according to the directions. Let croissants cool to the touch before cutting them in half at the center point. Once cut, the shape will resemble miniature "horns of plenty." Gently press or pull some dough from the large "horn" side of the half of croissant to create a cavity for filling. Set these aside for the moment.
- In a large mixing bowl, add in whipped cream cheese, shrimp sauce and ketchup. Lightly blend with a fork.
- In a colander, fully drain a can of miniature shrimp and one can of crab meat (pulled apart and loose.)
- After the fish mixture is fully drained, pour into the mixing bowl and lightly mix it all together with a fork making sure you don't break up the small shrimp pieces.
- Scoop up some of the mixture with your fingers to fill the croissant cavity making sure you pack in the mixture. A gentle push-in will do. Fill the cavity to the top and with a teaspoon scoop additional filling to form a round cap on the "horn of plenty" side opening. Once formed, place on a cookie sheet. Repeat until you have completed filling all the pieces. Sprinkle powdered sugar over the croissant section only and serve at room temperature.

Wine Pairing

A crisp, light white such as Riesling QbA.
SUGGESTION: Turn Me Riesling, a QbA Riesling from the Rheinhessen region in Germany.

Frezzelle Mini Combos

PREP TIME: 15 MINUTES SERVES 4

INGREDIENTS

4 mini frezzelles
white, wheat, or multi-grain

olive oil

balsamic vinegar

salt

black pepper

garlic salt

oregano

water

1 hardboiled egg

1 small can solid white albacore tuna

1 large tomato

1 small jar roasted red peppers

1 small jar chopped artichoke hearts

I was five when I learned how to make my first frezzelle at an Italian bakery in the old neighborhood. This crispy Italian twice baked circular dried bread with a hole in the middle may have originated in Puglia, Italy, but was at home on many meatless Friday night dinners when I was growing up.

PREPARATION: BASE STRUCTURE

- Whether you use mini or full-size frezzelles in white, whole wheat or multi-grain, the secret is to wet it down just enough to hear and feel the snap of the crispy surface with your thumb. Run the frezzelle under a spray of tap water in a circular motion on the top and flip it over and repeat for the bottom side. Place on a flat dinner plate flat side up.
- Drizzle olive oil around the frezzelle in a circular motion, then follow with balsamic vinegar in the same manner. Season with salt, pepper and garlic salt to taste. This completes the base of the frezzelle and now it's ready for a variety of toppings.

PREPARATION: TOPPINGS

This recipe calls for albacore tuna, chopped hardboiled egg, roasted red peppers, and chopped artichoke hearts.

- Drain the can of tuna and mix in a chopped hardboiled egg and sprinkle on top. Add more olive oil and balsamic vinegar to taste.
- Sprinkle chopped tomatoes, artichoke hearts and roasted red peppers on the other.

Wine Pairing

A light bodied, unoaked, white such as a Verdicchio.

Gen's Eggplant Caponata

PREP TIME: 10 MINUTES   COOK TIME: 35–40 MINUTES   TOTAL: 1 HOUR   SERVES 8–10

INGREDIENTS

- 1 medium eggplant
- 3 celery stalks
- 1 medium onion
- 1 clove garlic
- 4 tbsps. oil
- 1 14.5 oz. can chopped tomato
- 8 oz. can tomato sauce
- 4 tbsps. capers
- 6 tbsps. wine vinegar
- 2 tbsps. sugar
- 1 tbsp. dried oregano
- 1 4.5 oz. can sliced black olives, drained (optional)
- salt and pepper

Think of caponata as a kind of Italian salsa. It's somewhere between a relish and a condiment with a wonderfully addictive sweet, sour, salty tang that will make you forget you're eating eggplant.

PREPARATION

- ✦ Peel eggplant and slice into ½ inch rounds. Salt thoroughly and let stand for 20-30 minutes. Rinse, squeeze dry, and dice. Dice celery and onion. Mince garlic.
- ✦ Heat 3 tablespoons of oil in skillet and sauté eggplant for about 10 minutes. Drain.
- ✦ Add 1 tablespoon oil to skillet. Sauté celery and onion 5 minutes; add garlic and cook for another 2 minutes. Add tomatoes and tomato sauce; cook over medium low heat for 15 minutes. Add eggplant and cook for another 10 minutes. Cool.
- ✦ Skim off excess liquid and oil. Add remaining ingredients including salt and pepper to taste. Refrigerate. Serve with crackers or bruschetta.

Wine Pairing

A fresh, easy drinking white wine with floral, fruity aromas, yet a nicely balanced acidity such as Macebao/Muscat blend from Spain. **SUGGESTION:** Marques de Caro Blanco.

Hot Chili Dip

PREP TIME: 10 MINUTES **COOK TIME: 15 MINUTES** **TOTAL: 25 MINUTES** **SERVES 10**

INGREDIENTS

8 oz. cream cheese, softened
9 oz. can Chili No Beans
8 oz. shredded cheddar cheese
1 large package nacho cheese chips

Maybe it's the warm, oozy cream cheese; maybe it's the gooey tang of melted cheddar. This dish is sure to go quickly.

PREPARATION

- Spread cream cheese on bottom of 8" × 11" baking dish or pie plate.
- Top with chili and then cover with shredded cheddar cheese.
- Bake in a 350° F oven until heated through and bubbly—about 10–15 minutes.
- Serve with some crisp chips.

Wine Pairing

A nice medium to extra dry, sparkling wine with the typical yeast aromas and orange, pear and apple flavors such as a Cava (semiseco to brut). **SUGGESTION:** Mistinquett Cava from Rioja, Spain.

Italian Flag Crostini

PREP TIME: 15 MINUTES SERVES 8

INGREDIENTS

- 1 large French baguette loaf
- 8 oz. roll goat cheese, room temperature
- 4 oz. container prepared pesto sauce
- 1 small jar roasted red peppers, thinly sliced

The Italian flag colors of green (hope), white (faith), and red (charity) are tastefully joined in this easily assembled appetizer.

PREPARATION

- Slice bread into thin rounds and lightly toast.
- Spread goat cheese onto each bread round.
- Top with a dab of pesto.
- Garnish with sliver of roasted red pepper.

Beer Pairing

A delicious, wheat-style beer would be a great accompaniant. **SUGGESTION:** Collesi Birra Imperale Bionda, a Belgium style Italian craft beer from Apecchio, Italy. *Silver Medal at the World Beer Championship 2010.*

Paula Guiliano

Food represented the link to family and friends; it was a way of making a decent and respectable living; it was the elixir that fixed what ailed you.

My grandfather, Michael Guiliano.

Me (Paula) and my brother Pat.

I was in my 20's before I realized that being Italian-American I shared universal attributes, family traditions and peculiarities with all other Italian-Americans from ethnic-heavy cities such as Boston, New York, New Jersey, Philly, and of course Chicago. We shared a common bond distinct from everyone else like our Irish, German, Polish, Greek and Jewish neighbors who resided just blocks away from our section called "Little Italy" in Chicago. My grandmother, Pasqualina Guiliano, as well as my own mother, Josephine (Pacelli) Guiliano and my father, Carmen referred to these non-Italian groups as "MED-E-GONES". This was an affectionate term, but a clear distinction none the less.

My grandparents migrated from a small town just south of Naples, Italy called Marigliano, and settled on the west side of Chicago on Taylor Street. This was a street that later became infamous around the world for its reputation during the Capone years with prohibition, yet it also represented an ethnic-rich, large, Italian community that supported and protected itself from the world that surrounded it.

My grandparents' goals were to provide a better life for themselves and their children in the land of opportunity, but nothing came easy. They both had a strong work ethic and soon raised enough money to purchase a three-flat on Taylor Street, which became a deli as well as the family headquarters and homestead.

My grandfather, Michael, also started a fruit and vegetable business for my Uncle Augie on Halsted Street, where together, they made many early morning runs to the Randolph Street Market to buy fresh produce each day. By night my grandfather made homemade red wine, while my grandmother made pasta, strung peppers, and canned tomatoes for gravy among other tasks in preparation for the store's inventory the next day.

My Aunt Kay Guiliano. Circa 1930's.

As early as age five, I was surrounded by food, cooking, canning, and wine making. I fondly remember my grandmother who was babysitting for my brother Pat and me, dragging us over to the Italian bakery around the corner, to play an Italian card game in the backroom with her lady friends, as we played with the older kids on the flour sacks in the front of the store. Here, in this place, I learned how to make my first frezzelle. See page 10. Perhaps this was the beginning of my culinary curiosity.

By day, I was allowed to play on Newberry Street. The corner landmark was Philly's Hot Dog stand. This was the center of my universe, because I could eat all of the hot dogs and drink all of the Kayo I wanted each day for lunch. I watched Philly as he sat in the doorway of this peculiar space and chatted with friends, telling the same stories to anyone and everyone who would listen, as he peeled endless barrels of potatoes and peppers. These neighbors represented our extended family, and although these stories were repetitive, they defined these individuals and made them interesting characters.

This neighborhood was also alive with a variety of peddlers who combed the streets with carts selling everything from toys, watermelon, fish, nuts, coal, ice, and yes, even a person who sharpened knives and scissors. Each person had a distinctive yell, and we knew them all as we waited for them to come down our street each week, while we cooled off under an open fire hydrant on hot summer days.

This was our summer camp, until my parents migrated to the western suburbs to a town called Melrose Park, which was also referenced as 'Little Italy." The suburbs offered additional social and economic opportunities along with a strong catholic school system, in which Our Lady of

Mt. Carmel church, along with its annual Italian Feast celebration became the epicenter for the town and the Italian community. Further west, which seemed like the countryside to us, my father, Carmen, opened a chain of liquor and deli stores called "Unique Liquors" which opened up more experiences and challenges that were worlds apart from whence we came.

I liked spending summers with my grandparents, because they would allow me to help them make the homemade pasta, or macaroni as we called it. When it was time to make ravioli, my grandmother and Aunt Kay would lay down white sheets everywhere and dust them with flour in preparation for laying out the long strips of dough I helped to crank out from the "macaroni" machine. Perfectly shaped dollops of ricotta were carefully applied about four inches apart from each other before that final layer was applied. These preparations were precise as far as my grandmother was concerned, but I never figured out how much a pinch, or a dash was until I started making these recipes on my own as an adult.

Sunday is family day with my mother, Josephine, my brother, Pat, my father, Carmen, me (Paula), my grandmother, Pasqualina and my Aunt Kay.

My grandmother did not have sophisticated tools to complete the ravioli process, so she used a drinking glass turned upside down to cut the ravioli out of the dough. It was my job to go around with the fork to press the edges. I truly believe this exercise launched my appreciation for all things fresh and homemade at such an early age.

Food continued to be a central theme in my life. I remember waking up on Sunday mornings to the smell of frying meatballs and olive oil. There was nothing like the smell of meatballs, crispy Italian bread, and a pot of hot fresh gravy simmering on the stove. All of this tempted our senses and egged us on to dip our bread for a taste. This was the precursor to the Sunday dinner.

Although every evening meal was important, Sunday was a special day where you could be assured that all of the family and various relatives and friends would join us each week for a spectacular dinner, at 1:00 pm in the afternoon.

When it comes to food, I think Italians have a twisted, but marvelous sense of meal planning that I inherited and carried well into adulthood. For example, my American friends ate only turkey on Thanksgiving and Christmas.

I mean they had stuffing, mashed potatoes and cranberry sauce, but that was it. We had this too, but only after we served the antipasto, soup, lasagna, meatballs, salad and whatever else my grandmother and mother decided to make just in case someone didn't like the turkey. We considered the turkey to be the side dish.

As for dessert we always had an assortment of fruits, nuts, pastries, cakes, and homemade cookies, including hot roasted chestnuts. I wasn't allowed to drink coffee with my dessert as a child, but I could have some of my grandfather's homemade red wine in a special, tiny little mug. Go figure! Although my grandfather created his own brand, we had an impressive collection of European vintage wines in the cellar. We celebrated each Sunday meal with good food, fine wine and great conversations. All subjects were on the table, and after we broke bread with family and friends, you could be assured that you learned something new about a variety of subjects.

My grandmother, father, brother and mother celebrating my brother's birthday.

Food represented the link to family and friends, it was a way of making a decent and respectable living, it was the elixir that fixed what ailed you; so it was inevitable that one day I would somehow integrate food into my life in yet another interesting way. One of the many reasons for compiling this book with some of my relatives and friends was to preserve these great tasting recipes and to pay homage to them for shaping and influencing our lives in so many ways.

Although we shared a strong family tradition for our cultural heritage, with education and the arts playing a major role in our lives, it also provided a profound sense of an entrepreneurial spirit in our blood.

But, alas, it was food that was the intoxicating lure. It was food that fed and supported us, it was food that comforted and entertained us, it was food that educated and enlightened us. Yes, we were convinced that food cured everything. Didn't it?

So there you have it, a small snapshot into three generations of living, within a food-frenzied Italian lifestyle, and loving every minute of it.

Cooking is part science and part creativity: I've heard it said that when you master the art of making soup you develop an educated palate. Some chefs even consider this as *acquiring good taste.*

Paul Ropski

2

Soups

Charlie's Pasta e Fagioli Bianca

PREP TIME: 5 MINUTES   COOK TIME: 45 MINUTES   TOTAL: 45 MINUTES   SERVES 4–6

INGREDIENTS

- 1 pound uncooked pasta, small (elbows, small shells, etc.)
- 2 15.5 oz. cans cannellini or Great Northern beans
- 1 tbsp. dried oregano
- 1 tbsp. dry minced onion
- 2 tbsp. olive oil
- 1 tsp. garlic powder
- 4 cups chicken broth (optional)
- ½ cup grated Romano cheese
- crushed red pepper (optional)
- Kosher salt and black pepper

My Grandpa Charlie shared my love of beans and taught me this quick and easy recipe when I was 9 or 10 and could finally work the hand-held can opener. I still think of it as the "real" pasta e fagioli: pasta and beans, while the tomatoes get the day off.

PREPARATION

- Bring 4 quarts of salted water to a rolling boil in a large pot. Add pasta. Cook 5–6 minutes.
- Drain most, but not all, of the water.
- Drain and rinse the canned beans. (If you have the time, dried beans that have been properly prepared are great.)
- Add beans, oregano, garlic powder, and dry onion to the pasta.
- Add 4 cups of chicken broth, if you have some; 4 cups of water if you don't. Cook on low heat for 20 minutes. Salt and pepper to taste.
- Serve with grated Romano cheese and crushed red pepper.

Wine Pairing

A nicely balanced, medium-medium dry white wine with a fruity and smoked aroma such as a Pinot Gris from Alsace, France. **SUGGESTION:** Klipfel Pinot Gris Cuvée Louis.

Cream of Mushroom Soup

PREP TIME: 10 MINUTES **COOK TIME: 10 MINUTES** **TOTAL: 20 MINUTES** **SERVES 2**

INGREDIENTS

3 tbsps. margarine
1 small onion, chopped
¼ pound mushrooms, chopped
1½ tbsps. flour
1½ cups broth
1 bay leaf
freshly ground pepper to taste
3 oz. milk

This comfort food makes a great accompaniment to quiche and a side salad. The soup is a far cry from the canned clumpy mixture of your youth. It's simply delicious.

PREPARATION

- Melt margarine in heavy pot. Cook onion in margarine until transparent. Add mushrooms and continue cooking until tender.
- Remove from heat and stir flour into onion/mushroom mixture. Add broth gradually until blended. Add bay leaf and pepper and return to heat. When soup reaches boiling point, lower heat and simmer for 5 minutes.
- Before serving, stir in milk. Garnish with croutons.

Wine Pairing

For a creamier style soup try a good structured, dense red wine with lively acidity and dark fruit notes such as Pinot Noir. **SUGGESTION:** Lady Slipper Pinot Noir from Carneros, CA.

Escarole and Beans

PREP TIME: 10 MINUTES **COOK TIME: 20 MINUTES** **TOTAL: 30 MINUTES** **SERVES 4**

INGREDIENTS

2	bunches straight leaf escarole
1–2	cans white cannelllini beans
1	tbsp. olive oil
1	clove garlic
½	cup grated Romano cheese
	salt and pepper to taste

This was one of my Mom's favorite recipes that she called "peasant food"—an inexpensive depression dish when meat wasn't possible. Now I've spotted it on upscale Italian restaurant menus!

PREPARATION

- Clean and chop escarole. Cook in boiling water 7–8 minutes. Drain well.
- Heat 2 tablespoons of oil in pot. Sauté garlic (not brown).
- Add escarole and beans (with bean liquid).
- Add cheese, salt, and pepper.
- Simmer for 10 minutes.

Wine Pairing

A fresh white wine with good acidity and tropical fruit notes, orange blossoms and apricot. **SUGGESTION:** Aromo Viogner vintage 2010 from Maule Valley, Chile.

Vintage 2010 won Bronze Medal/81pts, Beverage Tasting Institute.

Irene & Joe's Vegetable Soup

PREP TIME: 15 MINUTES COOK TIME: SOUP 30 MINUTES, BROTH 2 HOURS TOTAL: 2½ HOURS SERVES 8–10

INGREDIENTS: BROTH

- 6 quarts water
- 6 celery stalks, roughly chopped
- 6 peeled carrots, roughly chopped
- 1½ peeled onions, cut in half
- 1 cup roughly chopped parsley
- 2 tsp. salt
- 3 bay leaves
- 30 whole allspice
- 1¼ tsp. whole pepper

INGREDIENTS: SOUP

- 6 quarts vegetable broth
- 2 quarts canned tomatoes
- 16 oz. peas
- 16 oz. peeled and diced carrots
- 8–16 oz. lima beans
- 16 oz. corn
- 16 oz. green or yellow beans
- 6 stalks diced celery
- 8 oz. medium barley
- 1 tsp. low sodium beef broth
- ¼ tsp. sugar

Wine Pairing

A lighter bodied red wine that is fruity and bright, such as a Pinot Noir.

SUGGESTION: Frey Vineyards Pinot Noir from Mendocino County, CA.

This is a delicious soup that tastes even better with fresh vegetables. It freezes very well so don't be afraid to make a large batch!

PREPARATION

- Combine all broth ingredients in a large pot and bring to a boil. Cover and simmer for 2 hours.
- Let mixture cool before you begin to mash. To mash, press ingredients through a fine colander or sieve placed inside a large bowl to catch all of the liquid. This will be cloudy which is fine as it reflects the coloring and flavor of the vegetables. Discard mashed ingredients as you will just use the flavored broth liquid.
- Add vegetable soup ingredients to the homemade broth mixture. When adding in the fresh canned tomatoes, include the liquid as well. Cover and cook for 30 minutes.

Homemade Broth

Josephine's Minestrone Soup

PREP TIME: 15 MINUTES **COOK TIME: 55 MINUTES** **TOTAL: 1 HOUR 10 MINUTES** **SERVES 4**

INGREDIENTS

2	large carrots
1	sweet onion
3	celery ribs
1	garlic clove
2	tbsps. vegetable oil
16	oz. can chopped tomatoes
1	package frozen spinach
2	cans chicken or beef broth
1	grated potato
1	can red or white kidney beans
1	cup frozen small peas
¼	cup fresh parsley
½	cup grated Romano cheese
1	tbsp. black pepper
1	cup small pasta

This is a quick meatless minestrone recipe my mother used to make that became a favorite within the family. It's easy to prepare and you can expand on the ingredients to match your taste.

PREPARATION

- Sauté chopped carrots, onion, celery, and garlic clove in 2 tablespoons of vegetable oil in a large pot. Add the 16 oz. can of chopped tomatoes and simmer until liquid dries, approximately 15 minutes on medium heat.
- Add in 2 cans of chicken or beef broth (low sodium) and two cans of water (using the tomato can as your measuring tool.) Cook this mixture for 15 minutes.
- Add in packages of frozen spinach, peas, and one grated potato and simmer for 30 minutes.
- Add in one can of red or white kidney beans, parsley, grated Romano cheese, and black pepper. Stir and simmer until mixture is hot.
- Add one cup of small pasta. (Cook in boiling water for 12 minutes, drain.) Then transfer into soup pot. Use small macaroni like ditacini or mini shells.

Wine Pairing

A medium-full bodied red wine with high acidity and firm tannins such as a Nebbiolo (Barolo or Barbaresco) or Sangiovese (Chianti or Brunello di Montalcino).

Lentil Soup

PREP TIME: 20 MINUTES COOK TIME: 45 MINUTES TOTAL: 55 MINUTES SERVES 6

INGREDIENTS

- 1½–2 cups dry lentils
- 1 can crushed tomatoes or 2 fresh tomatoes
- ½ cup olive oil
- 2 carrots, diced
- 2 ribs of celery, diced
- 1 onion, diced
- 2 cups chopped spinach or Swiss chard
- ½ cup grated Romano cheese
- ½ tsp. oregano
- ½ tsp. dried parsley
- salt and pepper to taste

Another favorite from the days of meatless Fridays! We never considered it the "health food" it has become today.

PREPARATION

- Bring lentils to a boil. Drain.
- Return lentils to a three-quart pot and cover with 8 cups of water. Bring to a boil and add tomatoes. Simmer.
- Heat the oil in a frying pan and sauté the vegetables for about 10 minutes, stirring frequently.
- Add the vegetables to the lentil pot and simmer for 1–2 hours.
- Add seasonings and cheese before serving.

Wine Pairing

A light bodied red wine that gives off hints of black cherry, plum, dark chocolate and tuffle mushrooms such as as Spätburgunder. **SUGGESTION:** Schlink Haus Pinot Noir from Nahe, Germany.

Nana Katie's Pasta Fagioli

PREP TIME: 10 MINUTES COOK TIME: 30 MINUTES TOTAL: 40 MINUTES SERVES 4–6

INGREDIENTS

- 2 15 oz. cans cannellini or Great Northern beans
- 1 6 oz. can tomato paste
- 6 oz. water
- 3 cloves crushed garlic
- ¼ cup Extra Virgin Olive Oil
- 1 tsp. crushed dried basil or
- 3–5 fresh basil leaves
- ¼ tsp. crushed black pepper
- salt to taste
- 16–20 oz. Low Sodium Organic Chicken Broth
- 1 pound small pasta shells or elbows
- 2 cups imported Pecorino Romano cheese

This was my grandmother's recipe which she prepared almost every Friday. It's a very hearty dish and easy to prepare for a quick meal.

PREPARATION

- Drain beans in a colander over a bowl and set aside liquid from beans.
- Heat olive oil in an 8-quart pot on medium. Sprinkle a few drops of water in the pot and if the water boils, the oil is hot enough to add crushed garlic. Use a garlic press. Then add in crushed black pepper, basil and salt to taste. Sauté for about 5 minutes.
- Add tomato paste and water and stir until fully mixed. Cook for 3–5 minutes.
- Stir beans into olive oil mixture. Cook for 5 minutes. Add bean liquid and bring to a boil. Then add pasta and stir for 5 minutes.
- Slowly add chicken broth until pasta is covered with liquid. Bring to a boil or until pasta is al dente. You can add additional chicken broth depending on how liquidly you would like the dish. Add in cheese to taste.

Wine Pairing

A crisp, white wine with good minerality and aromas of peach and citrus such a German Reisling. **SUGGESTION:** St. Christopher Berkastler Kurfürstlay Kabinett.

Nana Katie's Spinach & Beans

PREP TIME: 5 MINUTES **COOK TIME: 20 MINUTES** **TOTAL: 25 MINUTES** **SERVES 2–4**

INGREDIENTS

2	15 oz. cans Cannellini or Great Northern beans
10	oz. fresh spinach
4	cloves crushed garlic
¼	cup Extra Virgin Olive Oil
2 3–5	tsp. crushed dried basil or fresh basil leaves
¼	tsp. crushed black pepper
	salt to taste
16–20	oz. Low Sodium Organic Chicken Broth
1–2	cups imported Pecorino Romano cheese

This was my grandmother's recipe which she prepared frequently. She would also make this dish with escarole instead of spinach.

PREPARATION

- Drain beans in a colander over a bowl and set aside liquid.
- Heat olive oil in an 8 quart pot on medium. Sprinkle a few drops of water in the pot and if the water boils, the oil is hot enough to add crushed garlic. Use a garlic press. Then add in crushed black pepper, basil and salt to taste. Sauté for about 5 minutes.
- Stir beans into olive oil mixture. Cook for 5 minutes. Add bean liquid and bring to a boil. Then add between 8–12 oz. of chicken broth and bring to a boil. Lower heat to medium, add spinach and cook until lightly wilted. Top with Pecorino Romano cheese to taste.

Wine Pairing

A light, fresh and fruity white wine that provides an elegant bouquet to round out the flavors of this soup. **SUGGESTION:** St. Christopher Zeller Schwarze Katz from Mosel, Germany.

Paula's Chicken Soup

PREP TIME: 20 MINUTES   COOK TIME: 2 HOURS   TOTAL: 2 HOURS 20 MINUTES   SERVES 12

INGREDIENTS

- 2–3 pounds kosher chicken pieces: breasts, thighs, and legs with skin and bones
- 6 cups low sodium chicken broth
- 2 cups water
- 2 cups chopped carrots
- 2 cups chopped celery
- 1 cup chopped parsley
- 2 cups small cubed yellow potatoes
- salt
- pepper
- garlic salt
- 1½ cups bow tie pasta
- ½ cup Romano cheese

The perfect Jewish-Italian cure for the common cold, and a hearty meal for cold winter nights.

PREPARATION

- Wash chicken pieces and lay them out. Pat dry on both sides and apply salt, pepper and garlic salt to both sides of each piece and let stand for 5 minutes.
- In a large pot or Dutch oven, add broth and water and shake additional salt, pepper and garlic salt into pot and stir to mix.
- Add chopped carrots, celery, parsley, and potato cubes into pot and stir to mix ingredients.
- Place chicken pieces into the pot and push quantity down and around for even distribution making sure they are all submerged.
- Bring mixture to a boil and let simmer for one hour and a half to two hours until chicken is fully cooked and falling away from the bones.
- When soup is just about done, take a strainer spoon and gently remove each chicken piece and with a fork separate the skin and bones from the meat. Repeat for each piece. Transfer the chicken meat back into the soup pot.
- Prepare bowtie pasta separately. Cook pasta in boiling water for 12 minutes, and then drain well before transferring pasta into the soup pot. Gently stir to mix contents. Simmer another 5–10 minutes until all contents are evenly heated.
- Sprinkle some Romano cheese on the top and serve.

Wine Pairing

A dry, delicate white such as a Pinot Bianco or perhaps a Verdicchio.

Potato Cheese Soup

PREP TIME: 20 MINUTES **COOK TIME: 30 MINUTES** **TOTAL: 55 MINUTES** **SERVES 6**

INGREDIENTS

- 1 pound potatoes, peeled, cut into ½-inch cubes
- 2 cups water
- ½ cup chopped carrots
- ½ cup chopped celery
- ½ cup chopped onions
- 2 tsps. chicken bouillon granules
- ⅛ tsp. ground black pepper
- 4 oz. Sharp Cheddar cheese, shredded

This soup is the perfect remedy for a dark, cold January day. Top with croutons and this hearty dish will make a perfect supper.

PREPARATION

- Place potatoes, water, onion, carrots, celery, bouillon granules, and pepper in a large saucepan.
- Over medium heat bring to a boil. Reduce heat to low, cover and simmer for 25 minutes or until vegetables are tender.
- With immersion blender or food processor, blend until smooth.
- Return to saucepan and add cheese, stirring over medium heat until cheese melts. Garnish with parsley before serving.

Wine Pairing

A full-bodied red wine that is succulent and mellow, with lush fruit, ripe tannins and a peppery-spicy echo such as a Merlot.
SUGGESTION: Esterházy Haydn, a Merlot from Burgenland, Austria.

Stefania's Yellow Bean Meatball Soup

PREP TIME: 30 MINUTES **COOK TIME: 60 MINUTES** **TOTAL: 1½ HOURS** **SERVES 8–10**

INGREDIENTS

6 quarts homemade vegetable broth (see page 30)

3 quarts diced yellow wax beans

INGREDIENTS: MEATBALLS

2 pounds ground sirloin

1 egg beaten

3 slices finely diced white bread

¼ cup chopped parsley

1 small onion finely diced

salt and pepper to taste

INGREDIENTS: TO ADD TO SOUP

3 tbsp. white vinegar mixed with
2 tbsp. flour

½ pint half & half

My Grandmother (Nana) didn't have this recipe written down. She came to our house one day to make it and we had to watch her closely in order to record the correct ingredients! This is a unique soup.

PREPARATION

- Simmer fresh beans in broth for about 30 minutes.
- Roll meatballs and gently put into soup. Simmer—do not boil—for about 1 hour.
- Skim off any fat. Add salt and pepper to taste.
- Add vinegar. Mix 2 tablespoons flour to half & half (as in a gravy preparation) and slowly add to soup. Do not boil.

Wine Pairing

A red wine with good structure, acidity, a little pepper and some dark fruit notes would be ideal. **SUGGESTION:** Seven Artisans Meritage (red blend) from Suisan Valley, CA.

Paul Ropski

When I was growing up preparing a meal was a fun event. I can still remember my father making Saturday breakfast to the strains of opera being broadcast, "Live from the Met."

My grandfather, Chef Albert and my father, Joe. Circa 1940's.

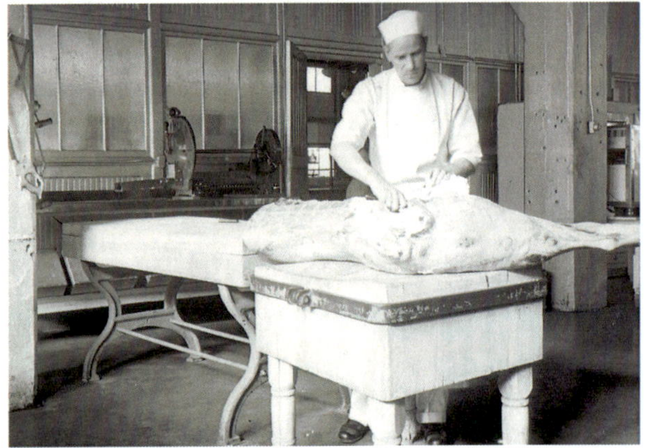

Chef Albert at work, circa 1940's.

What do you make for dinner on the nights that you don't "make reservations"? If you need inspiration, try some of our signature dishes.

Preparing and enjoying good food has always been important to my family. Whether it comes from their garden or from a farmer's garden, fresh fruits and vegetables are paramount. You might even say that we were "locavores" before it became trendy. By definition, locavores buy as much of their food as possible from local farmers in order to support their growing practices.

Cooking is in my genes. My grandfather came to America from Poland as a young man in 1909 to live with relatives in Connecticut before settling in Pennsylvania. After much hard work he established himself as an excellent chef at various private clubs, executive dining rooms, and hotels. My father still proudly displays an old newsletter from the local Press Club that encouraged members to savor a delicious meal in the dining room prepared, "the Chef Albert way." At home, my grandmother made most of the regular meals yet wasn't intimidated to cook for a chef! Unfortunately, none of his recipes were written down so there is no way to recreate Chef Albert's specialties.

However, my father does have his chef knives, which he treasures. You can see some of the knives in the background of the photo where Chef Albert is preparing to cut up a side of beef. Ironically, these knives still cut better than any of the other knives in my parent's kitchen.

My grandfather was very proud to be a chef and was always pristine in his crisp white uniform and toque (chef's hat). We often reflect how pleased he would be to know that my family continues the tradition of preparing good food.

My mother was also raised in a household that loved to cook and entertain. Her father was a physician and many of the medical auxiliary meetings were often hosted at their home. Why? The guests were always guaranteed a scrumptious meal afterward. Nana was a master at preparing filet mignon, (which was delivered fresh), in a cast iron skillet. You'll find some recipes that she liked to make including *Stefania's Yellow Bean Meatball Soup* on page 44 and the *Persian Salad Dressing* on page 68. She was a perfectionist and sometimes used my grandfather as her taste tester. The labels on her homemade chili sauce and jams were usually marked, "just right-Mel." This affirmed that he tasted a sample and it was perfect!

From left to right: My mother, Irene, cousin Mercedes, Nana Stefania and Aunt Evelyn at a 1965 bridal shower.

Cooking can also be competitive. As a newlywed, my mother baked the Polish kuch bread, (recipe on page 188) and shared it with relatives. My grandmother was visiting her cousins one day and they served some of the kuch. After sampling it she declared, "This is so delicious that you must give Irene the recipe." They smiled and said, "Actually, she made this!"

When I was growing up preparing a meal was a fun event. I can still remember my father making Saturday breakfast to the strains of opera being broadcast, *"Live from the Met."* My parents continued the tradition of good cooking and one of their favorite dinner party meals was prime rib au jus served with twice baked potatoes, salad, and at least two different local vegetables. The final treat was a selection of homemade pies for which my father made the crust and my mother prepared the fruit filling.

When my family celebrated holidays we often incorporated Polish customs. For example, the Easter dinner always began with food that had been packed in a decorative basket and blessed at church earlier.

As a prelude to the first course, the first item to share was a piece of a boiled egg which symbolized good health and prosperity. The other foods included the special kuch bread, butter in the shape of a lamb, fresh and smoked kielbasa, salt and pepper, slices of ham, beets mixed with horseradish, an egg that we personally chose, and perhaps some chocolates shaped like bunny rabbits.

The most sentimental meal is enjoyed on Christmas Eve. Before the food is served family and guests share in a piece of the unleavened bread called Oplatek. It is often an emotional event as this "bread of love" is distributed to everyone and heartfelt wishes are exchanged.

Thankfully, I never heard my parents exclaim, "Stay out of the kitchen." Instead, my brothers and I were invited to participate and learn how to prepare and present a delicious meal. As a young boy, there were even times when I'd concoct a meal, create menus, and serve my family. I pretended that we were dining at my version of a very fancy restaurant which I decided to name, *Shavoney's Port of Call!*

Besides developing the skills to prepare a meal, it was also important to learn how to enjoy it by practicing good table manners. My mother would tell us that when you have good manners, "You can even eat with the Queen of England and not be embarrassed!" I clearly recall the times she would get up from her chair to remind us to, "Sit up straight and keep your elbows off the table." Speaking of the table, whenever my parents entertain they still like to use their fine linens, china, crystal, and silver to enhance the experience. In the center of the table you will always find a holiday decoration or fresh flowers to complement the setting. As soon as everyone gathers around the table the last routine is to take a group photo.

Christmas Eve holiday table setting, 2010.

I invite you to explore all of the recipes included in *Life Beyond Takeout.* If you notice something that you haven't eaten before or that takes longer to prepare than your usual fare, be adventurous and try it. As my parents always said, "You may not like a particular food but you won't know until you try it." Bon appétit and I hope that some of these recipes will help you to create your own special cooking memories.

After preparing a homemade meal, there's nothing more rewarding than gathering together at the table and enjoying the company of good friends and family.

Jim Karagianes

3

Salads

Baccala Salad

PREP TIME: 3 DAYS COOK TIME: 20 MINUTES TOTAL: 3 DAYS SERVES 4–8

INGREDIENTS

- 1–1½ pound baccala (boneless)
- 1 jar giardiniera, mild
- 2 tbsps. fresh flat parsley, minced
- 1 4.5 oz. can sliced black olives, drained (optional)
- salt and black pepper

Before refrigeration, baccala—salt cod—was one of the most important food items in the western world. Its place in many cuisines has to do with its unique flavor and texture, though, not its durability. It's a Christmas Eve necessity in my house, whether fried, stewed, or in this easy salad.

PREPARATION

- Cut the dry baccala into 5–6 pieces, place in a sealable container and cover with cold water. Soak the fish for three days, changing the water 2–3 times each day. This will eliminate most of the saltiness and rehydrate the fish.
- When the fish is done soaking, bring 2–3 quarts of water to a boil, add the fish, and reduce to a simmer. Cook for 15 minutes or until the fish begins to flake.
- Drain and rinse with cold water. Cool.
- Using your fingers, flake fish into a mixing bowl. Add giardiniera (and olives) until the ratio of fish to veggies is about 4 to 1.
- Salt and pepper to taste; top with minced parsley. Serve with a crusty bread, bruschetta, or crackers.

Wine Pairing

A crisp, refreshing, slightly sweet white wine such as a Riesling Kabinett. **SUGGESTION:** St. Christopher Piesporter Michelsberg Kabinett from Mosel, Germany.

Broccoli Salad

PREP TIME: 10 MINUTES　COOK TIME: 20 MINUTES　TOTAL: 30 MINUTES　SERVES 4

INGREDIENTS: SALAD

- 2 heads broccoli
- 1 small jar chopped pimentos
- 1 lemon

INGREDIENTS: DRESSING

- ½ cup salad oil
- ¼ cup cider vinegar
- ¼ cup sugar (optional)
- ½ tsp. salt

This simply prepared vegetable found a spot on almost all of our holiday tables. No need to drown it in melted cheese; it stands up very well on its own.

PREPARATION

- ✦ Trim off the large leaves from the broccoli stem. Remove the tough stalk at the end and wash broccoli head thoroughly. Cut the head into florets. Steam until tender but firm, about 5–7 minutes. Drain well.
- ✦ Arrange florets on plate and garnish with pimento or lemon slices.
- ✦ Whisk together oil, cider vinegar, sugar, and salt. Drizzle over broccoli; don't overdo.

Wine Pairing

A refreshing, light, white wine with a soft finish, great minerality, good acidity and hints of pepper/spice notes such as a Grüner Veltliner. **SUGGESTION:** Mo-Velt GrünerVeltliner from Austria.

Caprese Salad

PREP TIME: 15 MINUTES SERVES 3–4

INGREDIENTS

- 1 Boston head of lettuce
- 1 cup olive oil
- 1 cup balsamic vinegar
- 1 tbsp. dried oregano
- fresh basil leaves (1 for each)
- 1 cup grated Romano cheese
- 2 large Mozzarella balls
- 2 large ripe tomatoes
- small container of Italian miniature black olives

For elegant dinner parties or just home alone, spice up your dinner menu with this salad creation.

PREPARATION

- Clean a head of Boston lettuce and pull the first set of outer green leaves off the head and toss. Each row thereafter will be a lighter shade of green and sweeter to the taste. Let stand to drain and dry then chill in the refrigerator for ten minutes.
- Use the leaves (approximately two) to create the base for each individual salad setup. Put them together to form a circular bed. Depending on the size of the head of lettuce, you may only net three or four setups at most.
- Slice a ripe tomato about a ½ inch thick and place it on the bed of lettuce as your first layer.
- Slice a thin piece of Mozzarella cheese from a large cheese ball and place it on top of the tomato slice as your second layer.
- Drizzle olive oil across the entire setup in a "z" shape, followed by balsamic vinegar. Then add a sprinkle of oregano on top of the "tomato/Mozzarella" topping only. Garnish with a basil leaf.
- Top with a sprinkle of Romano cheese. Garnish the lettuce base with miniature Italian black olives.

Wine Pairing

An off-dry rosé that displays some fresh fruit such as a Rosé from France's Languedoc (Cinsault & Carignan) or Rhone Valley.

Chicken Salad

PREP TIME: 15 MINUTES COOK TIME: 45 MINUTES TOTAL: 1 HOUR SERVES 4–6

INGREDIENTS

- 4 skinless, boneless, Kosher chicken breasts
- 1 cup mayonnaise
- 1 tbsp. mustard
- 1 tbsp. dill relish
- 2 tbsps. sweet relish
- 3 large celery sticks
- 1 cup red seedless grapes
- ¼ tsp. salt
- ¼ tsp. black pepper
- ¼ tsp. garlic salt
- water

Whether you are making a party dish or lunch for two, this recipe is easy to make and refrigerates well for up to four days.

PREPARATION

- Heat oven to 350° F. Season four skinless, boneless chicken breasts on both sides and place in a small baking pan. Add ⅛–¼ inch of water and cover tightly with aluminum foil. Bake for 45 minutes until completely soft and tender.
- Remove chicken and cut breasts into small chunks or cube size pieces then set aside to cool. Use a fork to tear the pieces apart so they don't look so uniform.
- In a large mixing bowl, add chopped chicken, mayo, dill, sweet relish, and mustard, and mix thoroughly.
- Chopped celery sticks very fine with an electric chopper making sure you don't puree the pieces. Add these contents into the mixing bowl and stir to mix evenly.
- Cut red grapes in halves then gently fold these into the mix and stir lightly making sure you don't smash the grapes. Cover bowl and chill in the refrigerator until cool.
- The chicken salad can be served as an appetizer by displaying it on a bed of lettuce or with crackers; and as a sandwich on your favorite bread.

Wine Pairing

A crisp, medium bodied, fruit forward white wine such as a Riesling Kabinett.

SUGGESTION: St. Christopher Piesporter Goldtröpfchen Kabinett.

Holiday Salad

PREP TIME: 20 MINUTES SERVES 8–10

INGREDIENTS

1	package Romaine Hearts of lettuce
1	large jar artichoke hearts
1	large jar roasted red peppers
2	small jars baby corn
2	cans of hearts palm
1	can colossal pitted black olives
2	large balls of imported Mozzarella cheese
8	oz. Italian dressing
8	oz. olive oil
½	cup grated Romano cheese
½	cup grated Parmesan cheese

The holiday salad is a favorite during special occasions, because it is hearty and beautiful. It makes a great first impression as your starter dish.

PREPARATION

- In a large colander, drain large jar of artichoke hearts and one can of colossal pitted black olives.
- Cut baby corn and hearts of palm into thirds and toss into the colander.
- Cut roasted red peppers into long strips and toss into colander.
- Cut large Mozzarella balls into thin slices and toss into colander.
- Drain colander thoroughly and then transfer contents into a gallon size plastic locking bag. Add 8 oz. of Italian dressing, and olive oil. Close top and shake bag to mix contents then store bag in a bowl in the refrigerator to chill.
- Clean and cut large Romaine Heart leaves into thirds. Let dry, than store in the refrigerator to chill. When ready to serve, add lettuce into a large salad bowl then pour marinated contents over the lettuce and gently mix. Sprinkle grated Romano and Parmesan cheese on top and serve.

Wine Pairing

A medium bodied red with high acidity, spicy and red fruit aromas, and very low tannin such as a Babera d'Alba.

Hot Spiced Fruit Salad

PREP TIME: 15 MINUTES **COOK TIME: 45 MINUTES** **TOTAL: 60 MINUTES** **SERVES 8–10**

INGREDIENTS

1	20 oz. can pears
1	20 oz. can peach halves
1	14 oz. can apricots
1	20 oz. can pineapple chunks
1	tbsp. brown sugar
¼	cup unsalted butter
½	tsp. curry powder
1	tsp. cinnamon
½	tsp. nutmeg

This dish goes well with ham or chicken and is easy to serve as part of a buffet.

PREPARATION

- Drain fruit and place in a 13" × 9" buttered baking dish.
- Sprinkle with brown sugar and dot with butter.
- Top with spices (which have been mixed together) and bake for 45 minutes in a 325° F oven. Serve warm.

Wine Pairing

A bright, fresh, citrusy, unoaked white wine would be a great companion. **SUGGESTION:** 3 Girls Chardonnay from Lodi, CA.

Vintage 2008 won Double Medal at the Lodi Intn'l Wine Awards.

Irene's Potato Salad

PREP TIME: 15 MINUTES **COOK TIME: 25 MINUTES** **TOTAL: 40 MINUTES** **SERVES 6–8**

INGREDIENTS

- 8 medium boiled potatoes, diced
- 1/3 of a cucumber, peeled and sliced thin
- 1/4 cup finely chopped chives
- 2/3 cup mayonnaise
- 3 tbsp. white vinegar
- 1 tsp. dill seed
- seasoned salt and pepper to taste

My mother would pack this on ice in a picnic basket for the beach to serve with her Sunday chicken. We enjoyed it and it was just how her mother made it. The cucumbers add a refreshing twist and this isn't overloaded with mayonnaise.

PREPARATION

- Peel potatoes and place in a large pot. Boil for about 25 minutes or until fork tender.
- Drain and cool potatoes. Dice the potatoes into cubes. Mix together all of the ingredients and add to potatoes. Chill and serve.

Wine Pairing

A well-balanced, slightly fruity, crisp, semi-dry white wine is a good fit, such as a German Riesling. **SUGGESTION:** Schlink Haus Riesling QbA from Nahe, Germany.

Joe's Italian Salad Dressing

PREP TIME: 10 MINUTES   MAKES 1 CUP

INGREDIENTS

- 2/3 cup olive oil
- 1/4 cup plus 2 tbsp. balsamic vinegar
- 1 tsp. sugar
- 1/4 tsp. oregano
- 1/4 tsp. basil
- 1–2 cloves crushed garlic
- 2 tbsp. grated Pecorino Romano cheese

When I was growing up we always had a cruet of this salad dressing in the refrigerator. I now make it regularly and the flavor is far superior to that of commercial salad dressings. My father shared this recipe with me and now I share it with you.

PREPARATION

- Mix all ingredients in a salad cruet and shake well before serving. Or you may mix it in a blender and store in a container with a tight lid.

Wine Pairing

A carefully made, not over oaked, Barbera d'Alba would be a good choice. This Italian, red grape variety is elegant, has a medium body and has flavors of sour cherry and spice.

Persian Salad Dressing

PREP TIME: 10 MINUTES   MAKES 3½ CUPS

INGREDIENTS

- 1 10¾ oz. can tomato soup
- 1 cup sugar
- 1 cup olive oil
- 1 tbsp. salt
- 1 tbsp. prepared mustard
- 1 tbsp. Worcestershire sauce
- 1 tsp. ground pepper
- 1 tsp. paprika
- 1 tbsp. horseradish
- 1 tsp. ground cloves
- 1 cup white vinegar
- dash of garlic powder

Why buy bottled salad dressing when it's easier and healthier to make your own?

PREPARATION

- Combine all ingredients in a blender and serve over a mixture of various lettuces.

Wine Pairing

A lighter and slightly sweet white wine with lower acidity, such as a Kerner (clone between Riesling and Trollinger.)

SUGGESTION: Schloss Koblenz Konigsgarten Kerner Kabinett from Koblenz, Germany.

Jim Karagianes

Continuing my family traditions is important to me. If I prepare just one dish that my Grandmother made, it's my way of remembering the happy times, which I still hold close to my heart.

My grandmother Katie celebrating her 91st birthday, circa 2002.

Italian and Greek cultures are rich in traditions. I have the good fortune of benefiting from the best of both worlds with an Italian/American mother and a Greek/American father. Although my father is of Greek descent and second generation, I had more exposure to my mother's family. That's because we lived a few doors down from my maternal grandparents, Nana and Papa. In fact, many of my cousins also resided on the same block. I visited my grandparents' home daily and enjoyed playing with my cousins. We also saw my paternal grandmother, "Yia Yia", a couple times per month for Sunday dinners. She lived in Greece six months out of the year and thus, we didn't see her as often. We would also visit her sister, Madeline, "Thea" (aunt in Greek), for dinner and holidays. She was an incredible cook and made all of the traditional Greek dishes, such as roast leg of lamb, pasticho (Greek lasagna), spanakotiropita (spinach pie), avgolemeno soup, tiropita (cheese pie), dolmades (stuffed grape leaves), etc.

We enjoyed these dishes on special occasions such as Greek Easter, considered the most important holiday in the Greek Orthodox Church. Although we did not participate in Holy Week Services, as we were raised Catholic, we did enjoy the Easter Day celebration of wonderful food and the tradition of dying hard boiled eggs deep red, to symbolize the blood of Christ. This was followed by a game among family and friends by holding one of the red eggs tightly in your hand with the point showing. Each person tries to crack the other's egg and the owner of the last uncracked egg is considered lucky.

Since we lived in close proximity to Nana and Papa, my experiences growing up were more Italian-American than Greek-American.

What do these rich traditions have to do with food? Everything! Life was centered around the table, whether it was for breakfast, lunch, dinner, or simply dessert. Sunday was the big day of the week at my Nana & Papa's house. This was the meeting place where all my aunts, uncles and cousins would gather for Sunday dinner at 3:00 PM.

One of my best memories is walking into my grandparents' house and smelling the fresh meatballs frying in olive oil. There is nothing better than eating a hot meatball right from the frying pan. Nana insisted on making 8–10 pounds of meatballs for Sunday dinner; three to four pounds just for people to taste when they walked in the door!How frustrating this must have been for the cooks, (my mother or one of my aunts), who were frying the meatballs. They couldn't make them fast enough for people to eat.

My paternal grandmother, Marianthe and her sister, Madeline, in a confectionery store my grandfather James owned on Southport and Addison.

The meatballs were only the precursor to the main meal, which always included pasta and homemade "gravy" (otherwise known as pasta sauce), which Nana prepared in the early morning and simmered for several hours. She also made breaded boneless chicken breasts topped with a variety of roasted peppers. Of course, there was always a large salad filled with Fontinella cheese and Italian cured meats, Italian bread and homemade wine.The Sunday dinner was typically attended by about 20–25 people. Nana hosted this event until she passed away at the age of 96. I cannot forget to mention that attendance was mandatory! If you were a no show, you'd better have been sick or have a good explanation of why you weren't there. Otherwise, you feared your next visit to Nana's house!

I have fond memories of many holidays at my grandparents' house, surrounded by family members and friends. Holiday dinners such as Thanksgiving included the traditional staples: turkey, stuffing, cranberry relish, vegetables, and potatoes. However, there was always an Italian touch to the meal, such as homemade ravioli, stuffed manicotti, lasagna or even another meat. No meal was complete without homemade cookies, cakes and pastries. My mother and all of my aunts are excellent cooks and bakers, which resulted in an overwhelming amount of desserts, (my favorite part of any holiday meal.)My grandparents' tradition of family gatherings with large meals still exists. But the hosts are now my mother and her brothers. Most of the major holidays, including the annual feast day celebration of Saint Rocco are hosted at my parents' home. And although attendance is not mandatory, it is expected! Just kidding, Mom!

It is better to have too much food to offer your guests than not enough. Welcome strangers and friends in your home and never bid farewell without a serving of food.

Fran Karagianes

4

Sides

Baked Beans

PREP TIME: 15 MINUTES **COOK TIME: 45 MINUTES** **TOTAL: 1 HOUR** **SERVES 6**

INGREDIENTS

2	28 oz. cans baked beans
1	pound bacon fried until crisp
½	cup ketchup
½	cup dark brown sugar
1	tbsp. hickory smoke flavoring
⅛	tsp. dry mustard
¼	tsp. onion juice
	salt and pepper to taste

This is the perfect side dish for your summer barbecue.

PREPARATION

- Mix all ingredients and transfer to casserole dish.
- Bake at 375° F for 45 minutes.

Wine Pairing

A wine with a little tanginess itself makes a good match, such as Zinfandel.

SUGGESTION: LaRocca Zinfandel from California.

Breaded Cauliflower

PREP TIME: 15 MINUTES COOK TIME: 20 MINUTES TOTAL: 35 MINUTES SERVES 4–6

INGREDIENTS

- 1 head cauliflower
- 2 cups seasoned breadcrumbs
- ½ cup grated Romano cheese
- ¼ tsp. garlic powder
- 1 egg
- oil

Of all the veggies that can be treated this way, cauliflower is by far the favorite of my family. It's the dish that doesn't get put away when the table is cleared, because, at that point, it officially becomes an after dinner snack.

PREPARATION

- Cut cauliflower into ½–1 inch florets. Steam for 5 or 6 minutes, and then cool thoroughly.
- In a bowl, mix breadcrumbs, Romano cheese, garlic powder, and black pepper to taste.
- In a second bowl, scramble the egg with a tablespoon of water.
- Dip each floret in the egg, let excess drip off, then place in breadcrumbs and cover completely. Place coated florets on a cookie sheet. When all are covered, place in refrigerator for an hour.
- Add corn oil or canola oil to a depth of ½ inch in a large skillet over medium high heat.
- When oil is hot, *carefully* add some of the cauliflower. Don't crowd the pieces—cook in batches. Turn with tongs to brown on all sides. Cook for about 5 minutes. Remove to doubled paper towels to drain. Add more cauliflower until finished. Salt to taste.

Wine Pairing

A lively, dry and crisp white wine with some fruit flavors and a mellow hint of white pepper such as a Pinot Grigio.

SUGGESTION: Tre Fratelli Pinot Grigio from Italy.

Calzone: Easter Sausage and Ricotta Pie

PREP TIME: 90 MINUTES (DOUGH MUST RISE) **COOK TIME: 30–35 MINUTES** **TOTAL: 2 HOURS** **SERVES 8**

INGREDIENTS

2 pounds Italian sausage
1 pound ricotta cheese, drained
8 oz. grated Mozzarella cheese
½ cup grated Romano cheese
3 eggs
½ tsp. salt
1 tbsp. black pepper
2 tbsps. dry parsley

My mother and my grandmother only made this calzone for Easter. I've never had it at any other time of year! What a special treat.

PREPARATION

- Heat oven to 400°F. Make a recipe of pizza dough (see page 86). While dough is rising (about an hour to an hour and a half) prepare the filling.
- Slice sausage very thin. It is helpful to bake sausage the night before, drain, and refrigerate. It is easier to slice when cold.
- Mix all ingredients in a large bowl. Refrigerate until dough is finished rising.
- Lightly oil and flour a 7" × 11" pan. Roll out dough and line pan with it. Make sure dough goes up the sides with some overlap.
- Fill the shell, evenly distributing the filling. Cover with a top layer of dough. Seal and flute the edges. Brush the top with beaten egg yolk mixed with 1 tablespoon of water. Puncture top with a fork, about 15 times.
- Bake for 30–35 minutes. Cool on rack. Remove from pan as soon as possible.

Wine Pairing

A semi-sweet, unoaked red with smooth structure and berry flavors.
SUGGESTION: Le Filou from France, a merlot blend. Try slightly chilled!

Carmella's Calzone Italian Rolled Pizza

PREP TIME: 1 HOUR COOK TIME: 45 MINUTES TOTAL: 1 HOUR 45 MINUTES SERVES 8–12

INGREDIENTS: FILLING

- ½ pound ground meat (beef, pork, turkey)
- 2 tsps. fennel seeds, crushed
- ½ pound ricotta cheese
- 1 large egg
- ½ pound shredded Mozzarella cheese
- ½ cup grated Romano
- ¼ cup Italian parsley
- 1 tsp. garlic powder
- 1 tsp. salt
- 1 tsp. black pepper
- 1 8 oz. can tomato sauce
- olive oil
- oregano

This is an extremely versatile dish. Not only can the stuffing include just about any leftover in your refrigerator (I've had it with hot dogs!), but it can be served hot, warm, cold and, I suspect, frozen.

PREPARATION

+ Make a recipe of pizza dough (see page 86). While dough is rising (about an hour to an hour and a half) prepare the filling.

PREPARATION: FILLING

+ Place ricotta in colander to drain.
+ Brown the ground meat with the fennel seeds. Drain thoroughly.
+ Remove dough from bowl and place on a floured work surface. Divide the dough in half and let the halves rest for about 10 minutes.
+ In a large mixing bowl combine ricotta, meat, Mozzarella, egg, Romano, parsley, garlic powder, salt, and black pepper to taste.
+ Preheat oven to 375°F. Roll out half the dough to a rough square of about 15 inches. Cover with half the filling, leaving a margin of an inch or so all around. Spread half of the tomato sauce on top of the filling. Starting with the side nearest you, roll up the pizza, tucking in the sides as you go. Place completed roll on an oiled cookie sheet, seam side down. Repeat with remaining dough.
+ Pat the tops of the two rolled pizzas with olive oil and sprinkle with oregano, black pepper, and a little salt. Slash the tops every inch or two with scissors or knife.
+ Bake at 375°F between 35 and 40 minutes until pizza is golden brown and a good crust has developed.

Wine Pairing

A medium bodied, spicy red wine with both fruity and peppery notes such as a Chianti or another red grape blend. **SUGGESTION:** Turn Me Red from Burgenland, Austria.

Louisiana Beans

PREP TIME: 20 MINUTES **COOK TIME: 35 MINUTES** **TOTAL: 55 MINUTES** **SERVES 6–8**

INGREDIENTS

- 1½ pounds total green and yellow beans
- 5 strips bacon, diced
- 1 diced small onion
- ½ tsp. pepper

INGREDIENTS: SAUCE

- ¼ cup unsalted butter
- ¼ cup sifted flour
- 1½ cups liquid from cooked beans
- 1 tsp. salt
- ⅛ tsp. cayenne pepper
- 2 tbsp. white vinegar

This is a delicious side dish that is best made with fresh beans.

PREPARATION

- Cook beans until tender—crisp—not too soft. Drain, but save 1½ cups liquid from the cooked beans.
- Sauté onion and bacon. Mix with beans and set aside.
- Prepare sauce by melting butter and adding flour to form a paste.
- Add reserved bean liquid and cook until thick.
- Add vinegar and cayenne pepper and simmer several seconds.
- Mix in beans and serve.

Wine Pairing

A Riesling blend, either a Kabinett or Spätlese level. **SUGGESTION:** Bauer Haus Späetlese from Rheinhessen, Germany.

Phyllis' Polenta

PREP TIME: 20 MINUTES SERVES 4–6

INGREDIENTS

- 2 cups Instant Polenta
- 4 cups Low Sodium Organic Chicken Stock
- 2 cups water
- 1 cup shredded Fontinella cheese
- 1 cup shredded Pecorino Romano cheese
- 1 Large onion
- 2 16 oz. cans drained cannellini beans
- 4 10 oz. bags fresh spinach
- 2 tbsps. olive oil into boiling water
- ¼ cup olive oil used for spinach and bean preparation

This dish is one of my favorites. My cousin Phyllis makes this dish in massive quantities for the Feast Day of Saint Rocco, which my family celebrates every year in August.

PREPARATION

- Bring water and chicken stock to a boil in an 8-quart pot. Drizzle in about 2 tablespoons of olive oil.
- Gradually add polenta in a steady stream, stirring continuously with a wooden spoon. Continue cooking, stirring constantly until the polenta comes away from the sides of the pot. This will take about 5–6 minutes.
- Lower heat and add one stick of butter, ½ cup of Pecorino Romano cheese, and ½ cup of Fontinella cheese. Stir continuously, until completely blended.
- Pour the cooked polenta into a 10" × 14" × 3" baking dish and set aside. Sauté onion in olive oil until translucent. Slowly add drained fresh spinach until lightly cooked, followed by drained Cannellini beans and cook for about 6 minutes.
- Evenly top polenta with spinach and bean mixture. Sprinkle a generous amount of Pecorino Romano and Fontinella cheese on top of the spinach and bean topping. Place into 350° F preheated oven until cheese is melted and lightly browned.

Wine Pairing

A light, refeshing and somewhat fruity white wine such as a Riesling.

SUGGESTION: St. Christopher Riesling QbA from Rheinhessen, Germany.

1 pk dry
1T sugar
3/4 C HOT
2T oil
2 C

Pizza Dough

PREP TIME: 90 MINUTES (DOUGH MUST RISE) **COOK TIME: 30–35 MINUTES** **TOTAL: 2 HOURS** **SERVES 8**

INGREDIENTS

1	package active dry yeast
1	tbsp. sugar
3/4	cup hot water
2	tbsps. oil
1	tsp. salt
2	cups flour

Imagine a childhood without pizza deliveries. Homemade pizza was pretty much a staple in our house.

PREPARATION

- Mix yeast and sugar; add hot water. Whisk until yeast is completely dissolved.
- Add remaining ingredients and mix well until dough is formed.
- Knead dough on a floured surface until smooth.
- Place dough in bowl, cover with towel, and let rise until dough doubles (about an hour).
- Grease the pan with olive oil using a paper towel. Flatten dough and press out to fit the pan it will be baked in.
- Layer on your favorite toppings and bake at 400° F for 10 minutes, then lower to 350° F for 10–15 minutes. When the bottom is slightly browned and the pizza looks bubbly, remove from oven.

Beer Pairing

You can create a variety of pizzas and pairings. **SUGGESTION:** Collesi Birra Imperale, Belgium style Italian craft beers. *Chiara, Rossa and Nera won Bronze medels at the NY Intn'l Beer Competition.*

Risotto with Cheese & Roasted Cauliflower

PREP TIME: 20 MINUTES **COOK TIME: 25 HOUR** **TOTAL: 45 MINUTES** **SERVES 4–6**

INGREDIENTS: RISOTTO

- 2 cups Superfino Carniola Rice
- 1 cup white wine
- 1 oz. Low Sodium Organic Chicken Broth
- ¾ cup Extra Virgin Olive Oil
- 1 large onion
- 3–6 leaves fresh basil
- 1 tsp. crushed black pepper
- 1 cup grated Fontinella cheese
- 1 cup grated Pecorino Romano cheese

INGREDIENTS: ROASTED CAULIFLOWER

- 1 head cauliflower
- ¾ cup Extra Virgin Olive Oil
- ¾–1 cup grated Pecorino Romano cheese

Risotto was invented in Milan in the sixteenth century. My favorite rice to use when preparing Risotto is Superfino Carnaroli Rice because of its creamy, smooth consistency.

PREPARATION: RISOTTO

- Grate cheeses then chop onion and basil and set aside.
- Bring chicken broth to a boil and then lower to simmer.
- In a large sauté pan, heat olive oil on medium, add onion and cook until translucent. Mix in basil and black pepper and cook for about 2 minutes.
- Add rice, constantly stirring for about 5 minutes. Make sure that rice is fully coated with mixture. Then add white wine until fully absorbed by rice.
- Begin adding stock, one ladleful at a time until completely absorbed. Only then is more stock added and the risotto should be cooked in this way for about 20–25 minutes, or until rice is creamy.
- Remove sauté pan from heat and stir in one cup of Fontinella cheese and ¾ cup of Pecorino Romano cheese, and one tablespoon of butter. Top with roasted cauliflower

PREPARATION: CAULIFLOWER

- Rinse cauliflower and cut in small pieces. Pat dry with a paper towel and place in mixing bowl. Add olive oil, black pepper and Pecorino Romano cheese. Mix thoroughly until cauliflower is covered with ingredients.
- Place on a jelly roll pan covered with aluminum foil. Preheat oven to 400° F. Place cauliflower on top rack of oven and cook for 20–25 minutes or until the tops are golden brown. Combine and serve.

Wine Pairing

A well structured, medim bodied, unoaked white wine such as a Chardonnay.
SUGGESTION: Aromo Chardonnay from Maule Valley, Chile. *Vintage 2010 won Bronze Medal/83 pts, Wine Enthusiast.*

Spinach Ricotta Pie

PREP TIME: 10 MINUTES **COOK TIME: 50 MINUTES** **TOTAL: 1 HOUR** **SERVES 6–8**

INGREDIENTS

1	deep dish 9-inch frozen pie crust
2	packages frozen chopped spinach
2	large eggs
1	15 oz. container ricotta cheese
1	cup light cream or half and half
½	cup freshly grated Parmesan cheese
	salt, pepper, garlic powder, nutmeg to taste

Believe it or not, this was a lunch box favorite for the years I worked. On my diet-conscious days I made it without the crust.

PREPARATION

- Cook pie crust according to package instructions for 1 crust filled pie.
- Thaw spinach and drain well.
- In food processor, combine eggs, ricotta cheese, light cream or half & half, Parmesan cheese, and seasonings. Mix well.
- Add spinach to food processor, gently pulsing until blended. Do not over mix.
- Pour into cooled crust and bake in 350° F oven for 50 minutes or until set.

Wine Pairing

A fruity, floral and herbal wine such as a Gewürztraminer. **SUGGESTION:** Klipfel Gewürztraminer from Alsace, France.

Sweet and Sour Carrots

PREP TIME: 15 MINUTES COOK TIME: 15–20 MINUTES TOTAL: 55 MINUTES SERVES 6

INGREDIENTS

- 2 pounds baby carrots
- 1 onion, diced
- 1 green pepper cut in thin strips
- ½ can tomato soup
- ½ cup sugar
- ¼ cup oil
- ¼ cup white vinegar
- 1 tsp. dry dill
- 1 tsp. each salt and pepper

Talk about versatile. Any dish that is as good hot as it is cold ranks high in my book.

PREPARATION

- Cook carrots in boiling water until tender, yet crisp. Drain and let cool.
- Mix soup with all ingredients except the carrots, green pepper, and onion.
- Boil soup mixture and pour over carrots, green peppers, and onion.

Wine Pairing

A bright, medium bodied, red wine with mineral such as a Zweigelt from Austria.
SUGGESTION: Esterházy Zweigelt Classic from Burgenland, Austria.

Sweet Potato Soufflé

PREP TIME: 20 MINUTES **COOK TIME: 60 MINUTES** **TOTAL: 1 HOUR 20 MINUTES** **SERVES 8–10**

INGREDIENTS

- 3 cups mashed sweet potatoes
- 2 eggs lightly beaten
- 1 tsp. vanilla
- 1 cup sugar
- ½ stick unsalted butter
- ½ cup whole milk

INGREDIENTS: TOPPING

- 1 cup finely chopped pecans
- 1 cup dark brown sugar
- ⅓ cup flour
- ½ stick unsalted butter

Here's another Southern specialty that is great for the holidays or any time!

PREPARATION

- Combine first 6 ingredients with a hand mixer.
- Pour into a greased 9" × 12" baking dish.
- Combine topping ingredients and sprinkle over the soufflé.
- Bake at 350° F for 35 minutes.

Wine Pairing

A fruity white wine, light and refreshing, with a strong body, minerality, and a little acidic such as a Sauvignon Blanc.

SUGGESTION: Ranga Ranga Sauvignon Blanc from Malborough, New Zealand.

Swiss Tomato Pie

PREP TIME: 20 MINUTES COOK TIME: 25 MINUTES TOTAL: 45 MINUTES SERVES 8

INGREDIENTS

- 1 unbaked 9-inch pie crust
- 10 slices bacon
- 1 large onion chopped
- 2 medium tomatoes, sliced ½-inch thick
- 1 tsp. salt, divided into ½ tsps. each
- ½ tsp. sugar
- ¼ tsp. pepper
- 1 tbsp. parsley
- 1 tbsp. flour
- 2 eggs, beaten
- 1 cup milk
- 2 cups Swiss cheese, freshly shredded

When the kids were small and balked at breakfast food, I would serve up some Swiss tomato pie—breakfast ingredients disguised as pie. Talk about a "spin".

PREPARATION

- Heat oven to 450° F. Cook bacon until crisp, drain, and crumble. Set aside in a large bowl. Pour off all but 2 tablespoons drippings and stir in onion; sauté until soft.
- Place tomato slices in single layer in same pan and sprinkle with seasonings using ½ teaspoon of salt. Cover pan and heat slowly for 2 minutes. Remove tomatoes and place in pie shell.
- Combine flour, remaining ½ teaspoon salt, eggs, milk, and cheese. Add to bacon-onion mixture until blended. Pour over tomatoes in pie shell.
- Bake in 450° F oven for 25 minutes. Let stand 15 minutes before serving.

Wine Pairing

A full bodied, semi-sweet white wine with floral notes, initial stone fruit flavors and a spicy finish such as Gewürtztaminer.

SUGGESTION: St. Christopher Gewürtztraminer from Rheinhessen, Germany.

Yellow Squash Casserole

PREP TIME: 10 MINUTES COOK TIME: 40 MINUTES TOTAL: 50 MINUTES SERVES 8–10

INGREDIENTS

- 2 pounds cooked yellow squash
- 2 eggs lightly beaten
- 1 cup grated Cheddar cheese
- 1 cup milk
- ½ stick of unsalted butter
- 1 cup diced onion
- 2 cups fine bread crumbs
- 1 tbsp. seasoned salt

When I first traveled to Texas I had squash casserole and loved it! It's a true Southern favorite and makes a unique side dish.

PREPARATION

- Slice squash ¼ inch thick and cook until tender.
- Mix all ingredients together.
- Bake at 350° F for 40 minutes.

Wine Pairing

A light, nicely balanced, easy drinking white wine such as a Pinot Grigio.

SUGGESTION: Moletto Pinot Grigo from Veneto, Italy.

Zucchini "Meatballs"

PREP TIME: 30 MINUTES COOK TIME: 30 MINUTES TOTAL: 1 HOUR SERVES 4–6

INGREDIENTS

6–8	medium zucchini
	sea salt
1	large sweet onion
¼	cup Extra Virgin Olive Oil
2½	cups Pecorino Romano cheese
2	cups Fontinella cheese
24	oz. Panko bread crumbs
4	eggs, beaten
1	tsp. garlic salt

My grandmother Katie and her sister Rose would make these famous patties once or twice per year. They referred to them as "zucchini meatballs", since they were formed in the shape of a fried meatball. These delicious "meatballs" were coveted by my family members and always disappeared very quickly. I have modified the recipe by using Panko bread crumbs and adding Fontinella cheese.

PREPARATION

- Grate zucchini and place on a flat cookie sheet and sprinkle with sea salt and let sit for about 15 minutes.
- Place zucchini into the center of white linen dish towel and squeeze out as much water as possible. Set aside.
- Sauté zucchini, chopped onions, and garlic salt until onions are translucent and zucchini is tender. Pour in beaten eggs into the sauté pan and stir quickly so that eggs do not scramble.
- Place Panko bread crumbs into a large mixing bowl and then add Fontinella and Pecorino Romano cheeses followed by the zucchini mixture. Mix well. Place into refrigerator for one to two hours or until firm.
- Remove mixture from refrigerator and form into patties. Fry patties in olive oil until brown and crispy. Remove and place on paper towels to absorb any excess oil.

Wine Pairing

A bright, white wine with just a touch of oak such as a Chardonnay.

SUGGESTION: Coloma Chardonnay from Sonoma, CA.

Zucchini Pie

PREP TIME: 20 MINUTES COOK TIME: 35 MINUTES TOTAL: 55 MINUTES SERVES 6–8

INGREDIENTS

- 3 cups zucchini, sliced and diced
- 1 small onion, chopped
- 4 eggs
- ½ cup canola oil
- 1 cup Bisquick
- ½ cup grated Parmesan cheese
- ½ tsp. marjoram
- 1 tsp. chopped parsley
- ¼ tsp. salt
- ¼ tsp. pepper

After a bumper crop of zucchini one summer, this recipe developed as a family favorite.

PREPARATION

- Heat oven to 350° F.
- Mix dry ingredients in a large bowl.
- Mix eggs and oil until well blended.
- Add wet ingredients to dry mixture just until blended.
- Add zucchini to mixture.
- Pour into buttered pie dish and bake for 35 minutes or until golden brown.

Wine Pairing

A crisp, lively, citrusy yet spicy white wine such as Grüner Veltliner. **SUGGESTION:** Mo-Velt Grüner Veltliner from Austria.

Vintage 2010 won Bronze Medal/84 pts, Beverage Tasting Institute.

Fran Karagianes

When you assemble a group of family and friends, you truly celebrate what life is about. I love to entertain and my home is now the "regular meeting place" where everyone is always welcome.

Saint Rocco statue, circa 1980.

My mother Katie, and me (Fran) celebrating my birthday. Circa 2005.

Daniel Burnham was one of Chicago's most famous architects known for his motto, "Make no little plans." As it turns out, my cooking philosophy is very similar! When entertaining, I always prefer to have too much food for my guests versus not enough. Nothing is ever wasted as I always offer them extra food to take home.

Every Sunday afternoon my family gathers together for a pasta and meatball dinner. See page 118 and take a bite out of my mother's homemade meatball recipe! This tradition began as a young girl when I would go to my grandparents' house for Sunday dinner. It was amazing how much food one little silver haired lady, (always clad in black), would prepare. Every meal was a feast and included homemade pasta sauce, Italian sausage, roasted peppers, meatballs, and fresh Italian bread.

We also enjoy celebrating many local feast days such as the one in August that honors Saint Rocco. This is a very big celebration for my family since my grandfather was one of the original founders of the San Rocco di Simbario Society in 1920. I host an outdoor party for about 100+ people every August. The guests who attend for the first time are always amazed by the abundance and variety of food. Sometimes the most popular part of the meal is the dessert table loaded with a selection of sweets.

My cousins also provide a very large table filled with hundreds of homemade cookies and cakes for the many participants of the religious procession. (See page 192 for Cousin Mary Ann's Chocolate Zucchini Cake which is an example of the delicious desserts served.)

As part of the procession, the statue of Saint Rocco is carried on the shoulders of the Society's members and is always covered with money offerings. These are pinned on ribbons and given by devotees who make special intentions for both living and deceased family members. Young women and men also carry a "chenda", or more commonly known among Italian Americans as the "candle house" for the entire procession. It is composed of hundreds of candles arranged in a multi-tiered wooden frame decorated with ribbons, flowers, etc. and topped with a small image of the Saint. The candle houses used to be carried on top of the devotee's head, but today the larger versions are supported by two or more people. As a young girl, my cousins and I would carry the candle houses. The procession includes two Italian bands for the entire length of the five hour walk. Firework displays add a festive touch to this Italian tradition.

Celebrating Sunday dinner at my grandmother's house. My father, Frank and me (Fran) on his lap, and my grandmother, Marianna to my right.

I also have many fond memories of spending summers at my grandparents' lake house in Union Pier, Michigan. Every summer, my mother, her four sisters, and my cousins made this annual trek. They happily prepared breakfast, lunch, and dinner for about 15–20 people daily. I remember that the day began with a large breakfast, which always included a frittata, (Italian omelet), homemade bread, pancakes, bacon, sausages, etc. We would then descend the stairs to enjoy the beach until about noon. We knew that it was time for lunch once we heard the large bell ringing at the top of the stairs. It was the perfect incentive for us to go back up to the house and gather around the two large kitchen tables in anticipation of a hearty meal. After lunch, we would play for several hours until it was time for dinner.

In retrospect, I can't believe the amount of work this must have been for my mother and her sisters. What a dedication of love!

From my home to yours, I wish that you also experience the warmth and love that comes from a homemade meal.

You like to eat;
you better learn to cook.

Bill Gorgo

5

Pastas & Sauces

Carmella's Cavatelli

PREP TIME: 1 HOUR 30 MINUTES COOK TIME: 15 MINUTES TOTAL: 1 HOUR 45 MINUTES SERVES 4

INGREDIENTS

4 cups flour
2 eggs
1 cup cold water
1 tsp. salt

Cavatelli comes in a variety of sizes, the longest being 8 fingers. My grandmother, however, prided herself on a one-finger version. Two or three sturdy index fingers gathered around the table will produce a batch of light, fluffy pillows.

PREPARATION

- Measure flour into bowl. Make a well and add eggs, water, and salt. Mix.
- Turn the dough onto a floured board and knead until smooth.
- Let the dough rest for 15–20 minutes.
- Cut the dough into four pieces. Roll out a piece about ⅛ inch thick. Cut dough into ½ inch strips and each strip into ¼ inch pieces. With your index finger, gently press down on each piece. Start at the top and move down toward the bottom, pulling your finger toward you causing the pasta to roll over on itself.
- Cover a cookie sheet with waxed paper; flour paper lightly. Put cavatelli on cookie sheet as they are made. Let dry at room temperature for at least 30 minutes.
- Bring a pot of salted water to a boil. Add cavatelli and cook 6–8 minutes until they are al dente. They are done when they float to the top. Drain and serve with a red sauce.

Wine Pairing

Enjoy your pasta with Marinara sauce over a medium-body red, such as a Chianti or Merlot. Meat sauces are best matched with full-bodied reds, Bordeaux or Pinot Noir.

Gravy and Gravy Meats

PREP TIME: 10 MINUTES **COOK TIME: 90 MINUTES** **TOTAL: 1 HOUR 40 MINUTES** **SERVES 6**

INGREDIENTS

1	29 oz. can tomato puree (see note)
1	6 or 12 oz. can tomato paste
2	tbsps. olive oil
½	cup fresh flat parsley, chopped
¼	tsp. garlic powder
2	tsps. fennel seeds, crushed
2	tsp. salt
1	tbsps. sugar
	black pepper
	red wine (optional)
½	cup fresh basil, chopped (optional)
	Romano cheese

Whatever it is elsewhere, in Chicago's Italian homes the red stuff you put on your spaghetti is gravy—NOT sauce. Tomato sauce comes in a can and you put it on pizza if you're in a hurry.

PREPARATION

Note: It's all about tomatoes. The recipe calls for tomato puree, which creates a good, basic gravy, but you can use an equivalent amount of chopped, crushed, or whole tomatoes. Each has its own texture and flavor profile. If you have the time, fresh tomatoes are great—just peel and seed.

- In a Dutch oven, heat 2 tablespoons olive oil. Add tomato puree (or equivalent). Reduce heat to medium low and partially cover to reduce splatter. Sauté tomatoes until very little liquid remains, 20–40 minutes. Watch carefully, stirring frequently to prevent burning. Tomatoes are ready when the surface looks like dozens of angry volcanoes erupting with a "pock-pock-pock" sound.
- Add tomato paste. Add four times as much water (just fill the empty can four times). Add parsley, garlic powder, fennel seeds, salt, sugar, and basil (if desired). Add black pepper to taste. Add any gravy meats (except meatballs) at this point.
- Simmer on low or low medium heat for at least one hour. Watch for the development of a foam on the surface as an indicator that the gravy is releasing some of its acidity. If gravy seems too thick, thin with water or red wine.
- Add a handful of grated Romano cheese right before serving.

Wine Pairing

A fruity medium bodied red wine with moderate to high acidity such as a Sangioveses.

Gravy Meat with Neck Bones

PREP TIME: 45 MINUTES **COOK TIME: 3 HOURS** **TOTAL: 3 HOURS 45 MINUTES** **SERVES 10+**

INGREDIENTS

12–15	pork neck bones
6	28 oz. cans tomato sauce Pagliacci brand
1	28 oz. can crushed tomatoes Pagliacci brand
½	tbsp. salt
½	tbsp. black pepper
½	tbsp. garlic salt
1	tbsp. dried oregano
1	tbsp. dried basil
1	tbsp. dried parsley
1	tsp. sugar
1	cup grated Parmesan cheese
1	cup Pecorino Romano cheese
1	cup vegetable oil

Italians make red "gravy" in a variety of ways using ingredients and various meats to create different tastes. Neck bone gravy is sweet tasting and leaves no bitter aftertaste.

PREPARATION

- Wash the neck bones under running water to remove any gritty bone texture and drain in a colander. Place in a large pot and add vegetable oil and brown on both sides. Remove each piece and lay flat on a paper towel and pat dry to help absorb the excess oil and juices from the browning process.
- There are many brands of imported and domestic tomatoes on the market today and each provides a unique taste depending on the type of tomato used and what region of the country it comes from. I prefer a plum tomato from the central and southern regions of Italy.
- In another large pot, add in the cans of tomato sauce, and crushed tomatoes.
- Add salt, pepper, garlic salt, dried oregano, dried parsley, dried basil, sugar, and grated Parmesan and Pecorino Romano cheese. Stir to mix these ingredients thoroughly. You can substitute garlic salt for fresh garlic slivers (approximately half a clove), but note that fresh garlic can overpower the entire taste if you use too much.
- Place the neck bones in the pot and push them down and around so they are evenly distributed and totally submerged. Cover the pot, and bring the contents to a boil then let simmer for three hours. Stir every 25 minutes.

Wine Pairing

A red wine with enough acidity to stand up to the acidity in the sauce such as a Chianti. **SUGGESTION:** Piertrafitta Chianti Colli Senesi D.O.C.G.

Lasagna

PREP TIME: 30 MINUTES **COOK TIME: 1 HOUR 30 MINUTES** **TOTAL: 2 HOURS** **SERVES 10–12**

INGREDIENTS

- 5–6 pounds ricotta cheese
- 2 cups grated Pecorino Romano cheese
- 2 cups grated Fontinella cheese
- 4–6 cups shredded Mozzarella cheese
- 4 beaten eggs
- 1 large bunch chopped Italian parsley
- 10–12 fresh chopped basil leaves, or to taste
- black pepper to taste
- 6–8 cups pasta sauce
- 3–4 8 oz. boxes Oven Ready Lasagna

The dish is believed to originate in Italy. However, the word lasagna is Greek in origin and is derived from the word lasanon, which means "chamber pot". The Romans borrowed the word to refer to cooking pots of similar shape and eventually the word came to be used to refer to the noodles.

PREPARATION

- Prepare your favorite tomato sauce recipe and set aside.
- Prepare the ricotta by draining it thoroughly in a colander, overnight.
- In a large bowl, mix the ricotta, salt, black pepper, Italian parsley, chopped basil leaves, beaten eggs, and 1½ cup(s) of grated Pecorino Romano cheese. Using a hand mixer, lightly blend ricotta cheese mixture until it's light and fluffy. Set aside.
- In a baking dish 13½" × 16½" × 4"), spread pasta sauce evenly over the bottom of the pan, followed by a layer of noodles placed in even rows so that it fits well inside the baking dish. Pieces should not overlap or touch side of baking dish since they will expand when baked.
- Spread an even layer of ricotta cheese mixture over the pasta surface followed by one cup or more of pasta sauce. You can also add crumbled meatballs (optional). Sprinkle lightly with Pecorino Romano cheese, followed by a heavy sprinkling of Fontinella and shredded Mozzarella cheese. Repeat process up to 5 layers.
- Cover with a layer of parchment paper followed by aluminum foil.
- Preheat the oven to 350° F, and bake for 45–60 minutes. Remove foil and parchment paper for last 5 minutes of baking so that cheese will turn a golden brown.

Wine Pairing

A medim bodied red with rich berry flavors and soft tannins. **SUGGESTION:** Spaghetti Red (blend) from California's North Coast region. *"Best Buy"* *85 pts, Wine Enthusiast Magazine*

Manicotti Stuffed with Ricotta

PREP TIME: 15 MINUTES **COOK TIME: 35 MINUTES** **TOTAL: 50 MINUTES** **SERVES 6–12**

INGREDIENTS

5 pound tub ricotta cheese
salt
black pepper
garlic salt
3 eggs
½ tbsp. dried oregano
2 cups grated Parmesan cheese
24–36 pre-made manicotti shells
4 cups pre-made gravy

See page 112 for meat sauce (red gravy) recipe.

Homemade manicotti is one of the lightest pasta dishes you will ever taste. Manicotti shells and gravy can be made ahead of time. Manicotti dough recipe can be found on page 120. Meat gravy recipe can be found on page 110.

PREPARATION

- Prepare the ricotta by draining it thoroughly in a colander. Use a fork to mix through it. For best results, drain overnight.
- In a bowl, mix the ricotta, salt, black pepper, garlic salt, oregano, eggs and one cup of grated Parmesan cheese.
- Lay out the manicotti shells in rows. Scoop the ricotta mixture onto the shell in a long row. Flip the two sides over the ricotta so it looks like a tube. Turn the tube over so the two flaps stay closed to keep the ricotta in place. Repeat until you make the required number of shells the recipe nets, which is 24 or more.
- In a large oblong pan, line it with gravy covering the entire bottom about ¼ of an inch high.
- Lay out the tube filled manicotti with the flap closure facing down in rows across and down until you fill the pan. Add additional gravy on top and sprinkle Romano cheese overall.
- Preheat the oven to 350° F, and cover with aluminum foil and bake for 35 minutes. Repeat with additional pans to complete the number of manicotti as needed.

Wine Pairing

A red wine with enough acidity to stand up to the acidity in the sauce such as a Chianti. **SUGGESTION:** Piertrafitta Chianti Colli Senesi D.O.C.G.

Nana's Meatballs

PREP TIME: 30 MINUTES **COOK TIME: 45 MINUTES** **TOTAL: 1 HOUR 15 MINUTES** **SERVES 4–6**

INGREDIENTS

3 pounds ground chuck
1 pound ground pork
4 cups grated Pecorino Romano cheese
8 onion rolls/buns
garlic salt to taste
black pepper to taste
¼ cup olive oil (for meatball mixture)
6 eggs

These delicious meatballs were a staple for all Sunday pasta dinners at my parents' house. My mother would usually make 6 to 8 pounds of meatballs in order to feed the 20+ family members who attended Sunday dinner at 3:00 PM.

PREPARATION

- Wet onion rolls/buns in a colander followed by squeezing water from them. Set aside.
- In a large mixing bowl, combine the meat with seasonings. Stir in the eggs. Add the onion rolls and Pecorino Romano cheese and mix well with clean wet hands. Make 4 holes in meatball mixture and fill each hole with olive oil (¼ cup total). Continue mixing until olive oil is absorbed into mixture.
- Form the mixture into either 3 inch patties or into 1½ inch balls.
- In a large heavy frying pan or skillet, heat olive oil and add the meatballs, rolling them often to brown them evenly on all sides. Place on paper towel to absorb excess oil.

Wine Pairing

An elegant, round, well balanced red wine with hints of spice, pepper and a touch of cocao such as a Spanish Crianza.

SUGGESTION: Marques de Caro Crianza from Valencia, Spain.

Pasta Dough & Manicotti Shells

PREP TIME: 45 MINUTES YIELDS 36 SHELLS

INGREDIENTS: BATTER DOUGH, MANICOTTI SHELLS

3 cups flour
3 cups water
8 eggs beaten
½ tsp. salt
plastic spatula
8-inch non-stick skillet
waxed paper

INGREDIENTS: HAND/MACHINE DOUGH, RAVIOLI, LASAGNA ETC

2 pounds flour
4 eggs
½ tsp. salt
1 cup warm water

Make a well with flour; add salt, eggs then mix in water slowly until it's all mixed together. Dust with additional flour to help knead the dough into a ball to keep it from sticking. Let stand in a bowl for ten minutes to rise.

Wine Pairing

A red wine with enough acidity to stand up to the acidity in the sauce such as a Chianti. **SUGGESTION:** Piertrafitta Chianti Colli Senesi D.O.C.G.

This is the most basic batter style dough for manicotti. It's so light you can eat three to four stuffed shells without feeling over stuffed.

PREPARATION

- Mix flour and water in a bowl with a hand whisk until smooth.
- Add in eggs and salt and mix will until you have a thin batter-like texture.
- Use a measuring cup with a pour lip and fill the cup with batter.
- Heat an 8 inch non-stick skillet over medium heat.
- Pour batter into skillet to form a pancake shape. The pancake or disc shape should be about an inch smaller than the diameter of the skillet so you have room to flip the disc over.
- The batter will begin to bubble over the entire surface, at that point use the plastic spatula to flip the disc over for a half a minute. No need to wait for bubbles to form on the second side. Place on a sheet of waxed paper to cool.
- Once you start this process, it will go very quickly so you will need to get into a rhythm on these steps: pour the disc, watch the bubbles, flip over, wait 15 seconds and remove.

Pastina with Egg

PREP TIME: 5 MINUTES COOK TIME: 10 MINUTES TOTAL: 15 MINUTES SERVES 1

INGREDIENTS

- ½ cup uncooked pastina (or acini de pepe)
- 1 tbsp. butter
- 1 large egg
- salt and pepper

Pastina with egg was my mother's version of chicken soup; it's what you were given when you had a cold, an upset stomach, a broken leg, or a broken heart. To this day, it remains at the top of my list of comforting foods.

PREPARATION

- In a medium pot, bring 2 quarts of salted water to a rolling boil. Add pastina and turn down heat to prevent boil over. Cook for 6 minutes.
- Drain most of the water from the pot—pouring about half of the pastina into a large wire strainer works well. Try to retain about ½ cup of water.
- Add butter and egg immediately and stir thoroughly. The heat of the pan, the pastina, and retained water will cook the egg, but do this over a low heat if you are concerned about the egg being cooked sufficiently.
- Salt and pepper to taste.

Wine Pairing

A crisp, clean, semi-dry white wine with balanced acidity. **SUGGESTION:** Weingut H.J. & E. Lehmen Estates Rivaner from Zell/Mosel, Germany.

Penne Pesto with Shrimp

PREP TIME: 20 MINUTES SERVES 6

INGREDIENTS

- 1 pound penne pasta
- 1 pound cooked shrimp
- 1/4 cup whipping cream
- 1/2 cup prepared pesto sauce
- 1/4 cup chicken broth
- 2 tbsps. chopped sundried tomatoes in oil

This fast, company-worthy recipe isn't exactly a diet addition, but the combination of tastes is hard to beat.

PREPARATION

- Cook pasta according to package directions. Drain.
- Add remaining ingredients. Heat and serve.

Wine Pairing

A fruity white wine with a strong body such as a Sauvignon Blanc. **SUGGESTION:** Arona Sauvignon Blanc from Malborough, New Zealand. *Vintage 2009 won 89 pts, Wine Enthusiast.*

Pesto Trapanese Sauce

PREP TIME: 20 MINUTES SERVES 4–6

INGREDIENTS

6 ripe plum tomatoes or
3 cups ripe cherry tomatoes

1 large handful fresh basil leaves, or to taste

1–2 crushed large garlic cloves

½ tsp. sea salt, or to taste

½ tbsp. black pepper

4–5 oz. Extra Virgin Olive Oil

½–⅔ cup(s) roasted almonds

½–¾ cup(s) grated Pecorino Romano cheese or cheese of your choice

1 pound pasta / your choice

This is an easy dish to prepare and very tasty. Your guests will be impressed as if you were cooking all day.

PREPARATION

- Preheat oven to 350° F and roast almonds on a cookie sheet for 5 minutes and set aside.
- Rinse tomatoes and pat dry with a paper towel. Place tomatoes into blender, followed by the basil leaves, crushed garlic, and almonds. Blend on puree setting for 3 minutes.
- Slowly pour in the olive oil in a steady stream, while the blender is still running, followed by ½ cup of Pecorino Romano cheese and ½ teaspoon of coarse ground black pepper or red pepper flakes (if you like a kick to your sauce), or to taste. Blend until mixture becomes emulsified. Place half of pesto sauce into serving bowl.
- Boil pasta until al dente, drain quickly and place on top of pesto sauce in serving bowl. Add remaining sauce to pasta and mix quickly. Add ½ cup of cheese and mix again until pasta is coated. Serve immediately or at room temperature.

Wine Pairing

A soft, unoaked, white wine with ripe fruit aromas and a creamy finish such as a Chardonnay from California. **SUGGESTION:** Mutt Lynch's Unleashed Chardonnay. *Vintage 2009 won 88 pts, Anthony Dias Blue's The Tasting Panel.*

Bill Gorgo

In my family, the true measure of the quality and quantity of food at any meal is this: how long it can keep people we love smiling, talking, laughing and eating at our table.

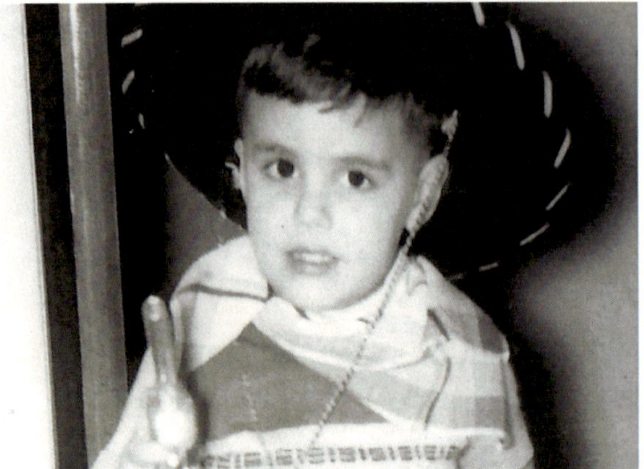

Cowboy Bill.

My grandparents, Carmella and Charlie.

One day, when I was 12, my mom told me, "You like to eat; you better learn to cook." Like a lot of parental advice, it was at once peculiar, excellent, and belated. Peculiar, because in those days men who liked to eat were expected to find women who liked to cook and live fatly ever after; excellent, because knowing how to cook has been and remains both a useful skill and a creative outlet; and belated, because my grandfather had started teaching me how to cook when I was 8.

Grandpa Charlie was a truck driver who, like many first-generation Italian-Americans, identified far more strongly with the country of his birth than the country of his parents. Grandma Carmella was an excellent cook of all things Italian, but she was often baffled by the dinner requests her husband brought home from his truck stop diner experiences: chop suey, corned beef hash, chili con carne, Boston baked beans, Spanish rice, pie à la mode, jello, rice pudding. Charlie was King of the Blue Plate Special and founder of the Sweet Roll Hall of Fame.

As soon as I was old enough to wield a can opener, I became Igor to Gramp's Dr. Franks-and-Beans. Fried red hockey pucks of canned hash with fried yellow hockey pucks of canned cornmeal mush on the side—yum. His experiments in fine dining were so redolent of his adventures on the road, beyond the neighborhood, out there in America, that they became associated in my mind with the cowboy tales we sopped up together at Saturday matinees. For my thirteenth Christmas, the last Gramps and I shared, he knew I was too old for the cowboy toys and paraphernalia that typically made his gift the highlight of the holiday; but he couldn't resist one last nod in that direction and gave me… a case of beans. To this day, my comfort as a cook has much to do with my tendency to view the kitchen as a glorified chuck wagon.

My parents, Genevieve and Joe.

If not for Gramps, my relationship with cooking might have been more like my dad's, a mechanic who enjoyed taking apart engines more than any chicken dinner and who could put them back together quicker than he could make a cheese sandwich. He was the black sheep of the dinner table: an Italian who didn't like to (over)eat.

My mother's cooking style could best be described as fatten-him-up cuisine; Pa's thinness seemed a visible, annoying critique of her efforts in the kitchen. After all, she came from a family where my Aunt Nancy would buy salami—this is absolutely true—to give away in case there weren't enough leftovers for people to take home *on Thanksgiving!* When I brought Lynn, my wife-to-be, to Christmas Eve dinner for the first time, my mother was so worried that the poor girl might not like the traditional fish offerings, she made a half dozen huge, stuffed double pork chops just for her. Welcome to the family: *eat!*

No one ever ate enough to please my mother; I doubt that anyone could. The game was rigged. If King Kong was coming for lunch, Mom would prepare enough for three King Kongs. First, she would complain that there was so much food left; then she'd announce that it would be a sin to throw it out; and finally, she'd ask if he would like just a little bit more. I learned how to cook for thirty by watching my mom cook for ten. One of the basic rules: prepare for the remote possibility that any one of the dishes you are cooking may, inexplicably, be the only thing anyone wants to eat. Another rule: there has to be a cafeteria's worth of choices in case, inexplicably, everyone wants something different than everyone else at the table.

There was a real advantage in watching Mom and Gram cook for armies of relatives. They never relied on recipes;

they relied on their knowledge of ingredients and of cooking processes. I hope you try my gravy recipe, but it really should be a video so you can see (and hear) what the tomatoes should look and sound like at various stages. And you'd still be missing the smells and little sample tastes (on Italian bread—why dirty a spoon?) every step of the way. The quantities of this and that are negotiable in so many ways, as long as you understand what each ingredient and each cooking process brings to the party. That lesson is best learned by watching and doing and that's how I learned—eventually.

When I naively asked my Gram for her pizza recipe, it led to a classic conversation—

Gram: First, you take flour.

Me: How much?

Gram: How much pizza you want?

Me: (after a long pause) Call me when you're making pizza so I can come watch.

I have never stopped learning about cooking, but the most important truth I've learned is the one that drove all the cooks in my family; the true measure of the quality and quantity of food at any meal is this: how long it can keep the people we love smiling, talking, laughing and eating at our table.

Cooking is about the care and love one puts into the preparation of food, whether one dish or fifty, whether feeding an army or fixing a midnight snack.

Geneva Gorgo

6

Main Dishes

Chicago Pot Roast

PREP TIME: 20 MINUTES COOK TIME: 8 HOURS TOTAL: 8 HOURS 20 MINUTES SERVES 4

INGREDIENTS

- 3–4 pounds beef chuck (bone in)
- 3 cups beef broth (low sodium)
- 2 cups water
- salt
- black pepper
- garlic salt
- 1 sweet white onion
- 2 cups baby carrots
- 1 cup chopped celery
- 2 cups red or white cubed potatoes
- 1 bag frozen small peas
- ¼–½ cup vegetable oil
- crock pot

This Chicago style pot roast is the "do very little, go to work for eight hours, come home and it's done" recipe. It's perfect every time, even if you have to work overtime for two additional hours!

PREPARATION

- Season a 4-pound beef chuck roast (bone in) with salt, black pepper, and garlic salt on both sides. Brown meat in a skillet on medium heat in vegetable oil until the meat is crispy on both sides.
- Heat your crock pot on HIGH. At the same time, add in the beef broth, water and the brown juices left from the skillet.
- Add in a layer of baby carrots, celery and potatoes, then add in the pot roast, followed by the balance of the carrots, celery and potatoes. Gently add in the frozen peas and push them down into the liquid so they are neatly distributed. You can't layer in the peas, because they will get crushed under the weight of the meat and other ingredients.
- Add in a sprinkle of salt, pepper and garlic salt overall and lightly mix these seasonings into the liquid. Make sure that all of the meat, potatoes and vegetables are submerged.
- Cut three slices of the sweet white onion and place on top of the entire mixture. Cover with lid and cook for 8–10 hours on high. No need to stir, and don't remove the lid until done.

Wine Pairing

A medium-full bodied red with high tannin content and a supporting fruit characteristic such a California Cabernet Sauvignon.

SUGGESTION: Rutherford Vitner's Cabernet Sauvignon.

Chicken, Artichoke Hearts and Capers

PREP TIME: 30 MINUTES **COOK TIME: 40 MINUTES** **TOTAL: 1 HOUR 10 MINUTES** **SERVES 4–5**

INGREDIENTS

10	ultra thin slices boneless and skinless chicken breasts
1	bag/box Panko crumbs
4	eggs
⅛	tsp. salt
⅛	tsp. black pepper
⅛	tsp. garlic salt
⅛	cup Parmesan cheese
1	bag frozen artichoke hearts
1	small jar capers
¾	cup vegetable oil
¼	cup olive oil
1½	cups water
½	cup Pecorino Romano cheese

Call this dish healthy and beautiful. This is a great dish to make when entertaining a small dinner party, or a romantic dinner for two.

PREPARATION

- Prepare two shallow pans for breading chicken by pouring Panko crumbs in one dish and eggs, salt, black pepper, garlic salt and Parmesan cheese together in the other dish. Mix egg mixture well before you begin.
- Dip each thin slice of boneless, skinless chicken breast in the egg mixture covering both sides, then into the Panko crumbs covering both sides thoroughly. Repeat for each slice and put them aside for the moment.
- Heat a frozen bag of artichoke hearts in a skillet filled with water over medium heat. Use a lid to help steam them until tender, approximately 15 minutes. Pour the water out of the skillet and replace it with olive oil. Season with salt, black pepper, and garlic salt and mix contents together. Simmer on low heat with the lid on until you complete cooking the chicken.
- In a second skillet, heat vegetable oil on medium heat then place the breaded chicken slices in the pan making sure they do not overlap. Brown both sides until crispy. Since the chicken breasts are ultra thin, they will cook fast. Remove the cooked chicken and repeat this step for the balance of your chicken slices. Browning a full skillet should take not more than 8 minutes.
- In the chicken skillet, add all of the chicken back in along with the artichoke hearts and capers (drained), drizzle with olive oil and heat until all contents are hot. Sprinkle Pecorino Romano cheese on top and serve.

Wine Pairing

A dry, peppery spiced and fruity white such as Grüner Veltliner. **SUGGESTION:** Esterházy Estoras Grüner Veltliner.

Chicken Breasts in Wine & Lemon Sauce

PREP TIME: 15 MINUTES COOK TIME: 45 MINUTES TOTAL: 1 HOUR SERVES 4–6

INGREDIENTS

- 6 large boneless, skinless chicken breasts
- 1 cup Panko bread crumbs
- 1 cup white wine
- 2 eggs
- ¾ cup Extra Virgin Olive Oil
- ¾ cup grated Pecorino Romano cheese
- 1–2 tbsp. butter
- ¾ tbsp. crushed black pepper
- ¾ cup freshly-squeezed lemon juice
- Low Sodium Organic Chicken Stock as needed

This is a simple chicken preparation which I also like to use as the base for my Chicken Parmesan.

PREPARATION

- Preheat oven to 350° F.
- Rinse chicken breasts and pat dry with a paper towel.
- Place chicken breasts on a cutting board covered with a sheet of waxed paper. Then place a piece of waxed paper over chicken breasts. Pound chicken with a meat tenderizer until very flat and thin. Set aside.
- Pour egg into a shallow bowl and add ¾ tablespoon of black pepper and ¼ tablespoon of sea salt.
- Place Panko crumbs into a separate shallow bowl and mix in Pecorino Romano cheese. Dip chicken breasts into egg, then into Panko bread crumbs.
- Sauté chicken breasts in olive oil until golden brown, followed by adding white wine until fully absorbed by chicken breast.
- Place sautéed chicken breasts in an 8½" × 11" glass baking dish. Pour lemon juice and chicken stock over chicken. Place a small pat of butter over each piece. Place in oven and bake for 20 minutes.

Wine Pairing

A semi-dry, fresh and crisp white wine with minerality reminenscence of tropical fruit such as a Mosel Riesling. **SUGGESTION:** Weingut H. J. & E. Lehmen Estate, Zeller Schwarze Katz Riesling QbA, Hochgewächs Halbtrocken, *84 pts from Wine Enthusiast.*

Chicken Parmesan

PREP TIME: 15 MINUTES COOK TIME: 45 MINUTES TOTAL: 1 HOUR SERVES 4–6

INGREDIENTS

- 6 large boneless, skinless chicken breasts
- 1 cup Panko bread crumbs
- 1 cup white wine
- 2 eggs, beaten
- ¾ cup Extra Virgin Olive Oil
- ¾ cup grated Pecorino Romano cheese
- 1–2 tbsp. butter
- ¾ tbsp. crushed black pepper
- ½ cup shredded Mozzarella cheese
- ½ cup shredded Fontinella cheese
- Low Sodium Organic Chicken Stock as needed

This is always a popular dish that pairs well with a side of spaghetti.

PREPARATION

- Preheat oven to 350° F.
- Rinse chicken breasts and pat dry with a paper towel.
- Place chicken breasts on a cutting board covered with a sheet of waxed paper. Then place a piece of waxed paper over chicken breasts. Pound chicken with a meat tenderizer until very flat and thin. Set aside.
- Pour egg into a shallow bowl and add ¾ tablespoon of black pepper and ¼ tablespoon of sea salt.
- Place Panko crumbs into a separate shallow bowl and mix in Pecorino Romano cheese.
- Dip chicken breasts into egg, then into Panko bread crumbs.
- Sauté chicken breasts in olive oil until golden brown, followed by adding white wine until fully absorbed by chicken breast.
- Pour Marinara Sauce into 8½" × 11" glass baking dish.
- Place chicken breast over sauce and cover with remaining sauce. Sprinkle Fontinella and Mozzarella cheeses on top and place into oven for 20 minutes.

Wine Pairing

A soft red wine with light floral aromas and a touch of earth as to stand up to red sauce of this dish, such as a California Pinot Noir. **SUGGESTION:** 3 Girls Pinot Noir from Lodi, CA.

Chicken, Snap Peas, Potatoes & Red Peppers

PREP TIME: 25 MINUTES **COOK TIME: 45 MINUTES** **TOTAL: 1 HOUR 10 MINUTES** **SERVES 4**

INGREDIENTS

- 2 packages chicken tenders
- 1 can shaker flour
- 4 large eggs
- 1 tbsp. butter
- ¼ tsp. salt
- ¼ tsp. black pepper
- ¼ tsp. garlic salt
- 1 tbsp. butter
- olive oil
- vegetable oil
- 4 large yellow cubed potatoes
- 1 bag frozen snap peas
- ½ bag frozen red peppers cut in long strips

Healthy and proportioned just right, this all-in-one dish is a "snap" to make with meat, potatoes and veggies using one skillet.

PREPARATION

- In a large skillet, heat vegetable oil and butter until hot, fold in cubed potatoes and stir continuously until soft and brown. Set this aside. No need to clean the skillet.
- In the same skillet, fold in snap peas and roasted red peppers and and add water and simmer with the lid on, stirring occasionally until all veggies are steamed. Drain water. Set contents aside.
- In a shallow pan, mix eggs, salt, pepper, and garlic salt and whisk thoroughly. Dip each chicken tender in the egg mixture until fully coated then in a second pan use the shaker flour to coat the chicken piece completely. Repeat this process until you have coated all of the chicken pieces. Set aside.
- Pour vegetable oil in the skillet, add butter and heat on medium heat until hot. Lay the floured chicken pieces in rows being careful not to overlap the chicken. Let the chicken pieces brown a bit before turning them over to do the other side. The process will take only 6–7 minutes. The vegetable oil should be fully absorbed by now. If not, drain it out.
- Mix the potatoes, snap peas, and roasted red peppers back in with the chicken and drizzle olive oil over the mix, than add additional salt, pepper and garlic salt and stir completely. Heat about ten minutes and serve.

Wine Pairing

A dry, peppery spiced and fruity white such as Grüner Veltliner. **SUGGESTION:** Esterházy Estoras Grüner Veltliner.

Country Meatloaf

PREP TIME: 15 MINUTES   COOK TIME: 1 HOUR 20 MINUTES   TOTAL: 1 HOUR 35 MINUTES   SERVES 4

INGREDIENTS

1½	pounds ground beef
2	eggs
½	cup ketchup
¼	tsp. salt
¼	tsp. pepper
¼	tsp. garlic salt
5	cups salted potato chips to be crushed

My friend Nita shared this favorite country style meatloaf recipe with me and it's the best tasting comfort food I ever had.

PREPARATION

- In a large bowl, mix ground beef, eggs, ketchup, salt, pepper, and garlic salt until fully mixed.
- In a second bowl, fill with potato chips and crush evenly to the size of breakfast flakes. Add contents into the ground beef mixture and knead in thoroughly.
- In a glass pan, mold the ground beef mixture into a football shape. Use a butter knife, and coat the meatloaf's entire surface (top and sides) with a thin coating of ketchup as if you were buttering toast.
- Heat oven to 360° F and bake. Do not cover the pan.
- Let the meatloaf cool off for ten minutes before you slice it.
- The meatloaf will look almost burnt on the outside, but it will be very moist on the inside. The baked-on ketchup makes a very crispy coating on the entire surface.

Wine Pairing

A bold and fruity, full bodied red such as California Zinfandel. **SUGGESTION:** Glory Days Zinfandel from Lodi, CA. *Vintage 2008 won Silver Medal/87 pts, Beverage Tasting Institute.*

Country Style Barbecue Ribs

PREP TIME: 10 MINUTES **COOK TIME: 40 MINUTES** **TOTAL: 50 MINUTES** **SERVES 4–6**

INGREDIENTS

- 8 boneless pork country ribs
- garlic salt to taste
- black pepper to taste
- 14 oz. barbeque sauce
- 2 tbsp. olive oil

Here is a delicious way to make barbeque ribs in the oven instead of the grill. This is an easy dish to prepare and very tasteful. This is a nice alternative to barbeque back ribs.

PREPARATION

- Place ribs in baking dish and season with black pepper and garlic salt, to taste. Drizzle olive oil over tops of ribs.
- Place in preheated oven at 450° F for 15 minutes and turn ribs over and bake for an additional 15 minutes, or until browned.
- Remove baking dish from oven, cover ribs completely with barbeque sauce. Cover with foil and reduce heat to 350° F and cook for 10 minutes.

Wine Pairing

A sweeter-style red wine with herbal characteristics, intense fruit notes, and flavors of berries, dark cherries and vanilla.

SUGGESTION: Turn Me Sweet, a slightly sweet, earthy Tempranillo from La Mancha, Spain.

Eggplant Parmigiana

PREP TIME: 25 MINUTES COOK TIME: 30 MINUTES TOTAL: 55 MINUTES SERVES 10

INGREDIENTS

2	eggplants, large
3	eggs
3	cups seasoned bread crumbs
¼	tsp. salt
¼	tsp. black pepper
¼	tsp. garlic salt
1½	cup vegetable oil
3	cups gravy (meat or marinara)
3	cups grated Mozzarella cheese

An Italian staple, the eggplant can be served as a side and for the main fare in a variety of ways from stuffed, sliced, grilled, fried, and baked. Add cheese and sauce (red gravy), and you have parmigiana Italia!

PREPARATION

- Skin and slice eggplants into ¼ inch round discs, then set them aside.
- Prepare two shallow pans for the breading process. In one pan pour seasoned bread crumbs. In the second pan, mix eggs, salt, pepper, garlic salt, and Parmesan cheese and whisk thoroughly.
- Dip each slice into egg mixture to coat both sides than dip the slice into the bread crumb pan and coat both sides thoroughly. Set aside these breaded slices, but do not layer them now.
- In a skillet, heat vegetable oil until hot on medium heat than lay in the breaded slices to fill the pan and be careful not to overlap them. Fry the breaded slices on both sides until brown and crispy. Pull each slice out and lay them on a paper towel to absorb the oil.
- In a baking pan, line the pan with gravy, lay out the breaded fried slices in rows, than apply another thin layer of gravy, followed by sprinkling pre-grated Mozzarella cheese covering the entire surface. You can add a second layer by repeating this process. Cover with aluminum foil and bake at 350° F for 20 minutes.

Wine Pairing

A softer, light and fruity red like a Grenache from Côte du Rhone.

Irene's Sunday Chicken

PREP TIME: 20 MINUTES COOK TIME: 1 HOUR TOTAL: 1 HOUR 20 MINUTES SERVES 6

INGREDIENTS

- ⅔ cup flour
- 1 tsp. seasoned salt
- 1 tsp. garlic powder
- 1 tsp. marjoram
- ¼ cup diced fresh parsley
- ⅓ cup grated Pecorino Romano cheese
- pepper to taste
- 1 chicken bouillon cube
- 1 cup hot water to dissolve bouillon
- 6 chicken breasts

This was a dish that my mother often made on Sundays. The aroma of the searing chicken always smelled delicious!

PREPARATION

- Wash chicken breasts and pat dry but still keep them moist.
- Combine flour and spices and dip chicken into mixture.
- Coat bottom of skillet with olive oil and lightly brown chicken on both sides.
- Remove chicken from pan and deglaze the skillet by adding bouillon mixture.
- Place chicken in 9" × 12" baking dish, pour sauce from skillet over it, and cover tightly with foil.
- Roast at 350° F for one hour.

Wine Pairing

A medium to full bodied white wine with some minerality and herbaceousness such as a Loire Valley style Sauvignon Blanc.

SUGGESTION: Nittnaus Sauvignon Blanc from Burgenland, Austria.

Italian Breaded Pork Chops

PREP TIME: 20 MINUTES **COOK TIME: 1 HOUR 20 MINUTES** **TOTAL: 1 HOUR 40 MINUTES** **SERVES 4**

INGREDIENTS

- 8 center cut pork chops, ½ to ¾-inch thickness each
- 3 large eggs
- ¼ cup milk
- ¼ tsp. salt
- ¼ tsp. black pepper
- ¼ tsp. garlic salt
- ¼ cup Parmesan cheese
- 4 cups seasoned Italian bread crumbs, Cento brand
- aluminum foil

Simple, tender and crispy; pork lovers will marvel at how soft these chops become, while maintaining their seasoned crispy taste.

PREPARATION

- For best results, use center cut pork chops approximately ½ to ¾-inch in thickness per each. You should prepare approximately two chops per person.
- Prepare two shallow pans for the breading process. In one pan fill with seasoned Italian bread crumbs, and in the second pan mix three eggs, milk, salt, pepper, garlic salt, and Parmesan cheese and whisk thoroughly.
- Layout the pork chops and pat dry on both sides with a paper towel. Begin the breading process by dipping one pork chop at a time into the egg mixture until both sides are coated, then into the crumb mix making sure you cover the entire surface and sides with crumbs. Repeat this process until you have breaded all of the chops.
- In a large skillet, heat vegetable oil on medium heat until hot, then add in your pork chops making sure you do not overlap the chops. Brown thoroughly on one side before you turn them over to brown the second side. This will prevent the breading from coming off. Remove them when done and lay on a paper towel.
- Pre-heat oven to 350° F, and in a large aluminum pan, spray cooking oil on the bottom, then lay out your crispy chops alternating top to bottom so you can fit a lot of them into the pan. Cover tightly with aluminum foil and bake for one hour.

Wine Pairing

A dry, peppery spiced and fruity white such as a Ries. **SUGGESTION:** Esterházy Estoras Grüner Veltliner.

Italian Meatloaf

PREP TIME: 20 MINUTES COOK TIME: 40 MINUTES TOTAL: 1 HOUR SERVES 6

INGREDIENTS

- 1½ pounds ground beef
- ½ cup dried bread crumbs
- 1 egg
- 1 tbsp. dry mustard
- 2 tsps. salt
- ½ tsp. black pepper
- 6 oz. Mozzarella cheese, thinly sliced
- ⅛ cup dried parsley
- ¾ cup ketchup
- ¾ cup water
- 1 tsps. Worcestershire sauce

This is not your mother's meatloaf. The addition of mozzarella cheese gives this dish extra juiciness.

PREPARATION

- Preheat oven to 375° F. Mix meat, bread crumbs, egg, dry mustard, salt, and pepper in bowl.
- Place mixture on a sheet of waxed paper and form into a flat rectangle.
- Layer cheese on top of meat mixture and sprinkle with parsley.
- Using the waxed paper, gently roll into a cylinder shape and place seam downside down in 9" × 13" baking dish.
- Bake until meatloaf is brown on top—about 20 minutes.
- While meatloaf is browning, mix remaining ingredients. Pour sauce over browned meat and continue baking until done—about 40 minutes.

Wine Pairing

A medium, hebaceous, red wine with notes of pepper and red berry and nice, round tannins. **SUGGESTION:** Aromo Carménère from Maule Valley, Chile. *Vintage 2009 won Silver Medal/88 pts, Beverage Tasting Institute.*

Italian Sausage with Melrose Peppers

PREP TIME: 15 MINUTES COOK TIME: 25 MINUTES TOTAL: 40 MINUTES SERVES 6–8

INGREDIENTS

- 2 pounds Italian sausage, mild or hot
- 2 dozen Melrose peppers
- 1 tbsp. dry oregano
- 1/4 tsp. garlic powder
- salt and black pepper

Italian sausage and peppers are a perfect pair. Strips of red and green bell peppers will do, but for a month or two each summer, Melrose peppers can't be beat.

PREPARATION

- Remove the stem end of the peppers, retaining the core of seeds if possible. Score the cut end of each pepper with an "x" to prevent the seed core from exploding!
- Cut sausage into 6-inch portions and pierce each one several times with a fork to prevent the cases from breaking.
- In a large skillet over medium high heat, add 2 tablespoons of olive oil and then the sausages. Sear one side. Turn sausages over and add the peppers to the pan. Allow the peppers to develop a little char. Turn down heat to medium and continue to cook until the sausage is completely done (about 20 minutes total). Alternatively, the sausage can be cooked on a grill and added to the pan when the peppers are done.
- Season with oregano and garlic powder; salt and pepper to taste. Serve in split lengths of French bread.

Beer Pairing

Handcrafted beer such as Collesi Imperale Birra Rossa, a naturally fermented Red Ale with an intense, pleasantly sweet and spicy aroma of caramel, malt and hazelnuts.

Nana Katie's Chop Suey

PREP TIME: 45 MINUTES COOK TIME: 30 MINUTES TOTAL: 1 HOUR 15 MINUTES SERVES 4–6

INGREDIENTS

6	pounds pork tenderloin
1	6 oz. molasses
16	oz. dark corn syrup
½	cup low sodium soy sauce
2	large onions
3–6	stalks celery
16	oz. Low Sodium Organic Chicken Stock
3	tsp. corn starch
¾	cup water
2	tbsps. canola oil
	chow mein noodles

This is my mother's recipe which she enjoyed preparing for our weekly Wednesday family dinners.

PREPARATION

- Cut pork into ½ to ¾-inch thick cubes.
- Marinate overnight in 16 ounces of dark corn syrup, 3 tablespoons of molasses, and ½ cup soy sauce.
- Sauté diced onions and celery in 2 tablespoons of canola oil. Set aside.
- Place pork in a Dutch oven and cook at medium heat until pork is no longer pink. Add remainder of molasses (4½ oz.) and additional soy sauce to taste.
- Pour chicken stock into Dutch oven completely covering pork and continue cooking.
- In a measuring cup, add 2 tablespoons of cornstarch to ¾ cup of water and quickly whisk. Slowly add into chop suey, constantly stirring to avoid any lumps. Continue stirring until sauce begins to thicken. Add additional corn starch to desired consistency.
- Add sautéed celery and onion, cover and cook at low heat for about 10–15 minutes.
- Serve on a bed of white rice and top with chow mein noodles.

Wine Pairing

A refreshing, light, sweeter-style white wine with great aromatics and hints of tropical fruits and berries, like a Kerner from Mosel, Germany. **SUGGESTION:** Weingut H.J. & E. Lehmen, Kerner QbA, Mosel, Germany. *Gold Medal, 90 pts Wine Enthusiast.*

Polish Kielbasa with Sauerkraut

PREP TIME: 15 MINUTES COOK TIME: 30 MINUTES TOTAL: 45 MINUTES SERVES 8–10

INGREDIENTS

2	pounds sauerkraut drained
3	bay leaves
15	whole allspice
1	small diced onion
3	stalks diced celery and leaves
1/4	tsp. sugar
	pepper to taste
1/2	tsp. Greek oregano
1/4	tsp. thyme
2	pounds Polish kielbasa
4	medium potatoes peeled and sliced

This is a dish that my mother made primarily for my father and brother. They enjoyed it the most but she wasn't as fond of it! Imagine cooking something that is good but not one of your favorite things to eat!

PREPARATION

- Place sauerkraut and all ingredients except kielbasa and potatoes in large Dutch oven.
- Cook on medium heat for 1 hour.
- Place kielbasa on bottom, arrange sauerkraut over it, and top with the peeled sliced potatoes.
- Cover and cook until potatoes are tender and kielbasa is done, about 30 minutes.

Wine Pairing

A traditional, slight sweet Hungarian red wine such as Blaufränkisch. **SUGGESTION:** Schloss Koblenz Blaufränkisch Sweet Red from Hungary.

Pork Chops & Sliced Potatoes

PREP TIME: 10 MINUTES   COOK TIME: 45 MINUTES   TOTAL: 55 MINUTES   SERVES 4–6

INGREDIENTS

6 pork chops (bone in or boneless)
8 red potatoes
1 large onion
2 14.5-oz. cans diced tomatoes
garlic salt to taste
coarse black pepper to taste
½ tbsp. olive oil

This is a recipe that I have been making for many years, which I have always enjoyed preparing for my family.

PREPARATION

- Place sliced potatoes into a 9" × 12" baking dish sprinkled with olive oil, followed by a layer of sliced onions. Top with garlic salt and black pepper, to taste. Set aside.
- Fry pork chops in a skillet until light brown on both sides.
- Place pork chops and drippings on top of sliced onions and potatoes.
- Pour two cans of diced tomatoes on top of pork chops. Sprinkle with garlic salt and black pepper. Cover with foil and bake for 45 minutes in a preheated oven at 350° F.

Wine Pairing

A medium bodied red with aromas of nuts, pepper and clove; flavors of dark fruits, and a hint of sweet oak such as Pinot Noir from Oregon. **SUGGESTION:** Iris Hill Pinot Noir.

Roast Leg of Lamb

PREP TIME: 20 MINUTES **COOK TIME: 1 HOUR 45 MINUTES** **TOTAL: 2 HOURS 5 MINUTES** **SERVES 8–10**

INGREDIENTS

1	6 pound leg of lamb (bone in or boneless)
4–6	garlic cloves
1	cup lemon juice
1	cup red wine
16	oz. Low Sodium Organic Chicken Stock
	lemon pepper to taste
½	large white onion
1	lemon

This Greek dish is a standard for my family during the Easter holiday.

PREPARATION

- Place lamb in a roasting pan. Make 4 slits on top of leg of lamb and insert a whole peeled garlic clove into each slit.
- Pour one cup of lemon juice and one cup of red wine over entire leg of lamb. Rub with a lemon pepper seasoning. Pour one cup of chicken stock in pan. Place sliced lemons on top of lamb and slices of one ½ onion across top. Marinate overnight in the refrigerator.
- Remove lamb from refrigerator and let stand for 30 minutes to bring the lamb closer to room temperature.
- Arrange lamb in roasting pan fattiest side up, so while the lamb is cooking the fat will melt into the meat. Insert a meat thermometer into the thickest part of the roast, not touching the bone if your roast is bone-in.
- Roast in preheated oven set at 425° F. Cook for 30–45 minutes or until lamb is browned and crusty.
- Lower temperature to 350° F and roast for an additional hour or until thermometer reaches 180° F, at which time lamb is cooked. Periodically add chicken stock to bottom of roasting pan, so that drippings fall into liquid, instead of burning in the hot pan.
- Let stand for 15–20 minutes before cutting. While the roast is resting, scrape up the drippings in the roasting pan to make a gravy, or use drippings themselves to serve with the lamb.

G

Wine Pairing

A full bodied, oak aged red with a spicy characteristic and intense berry aromas such as Blaufränkisch-Cabernet Sauv. Blend.
SUGGESTION: Esterházy Estoras Red from Burgenland, Austria. *Vintage 2009 won 92pts & was "Cellar Selection", Wine Enthusiast.*

Stuffed Calamari

PREP TIME: 30 MINUTES COOK TIME: 30 MINUTES TOTAL: 1 HOUR SERVES 6

INGREDIENTS

- 3 pounds small (3–6 inch) squid, cleaned
- 2 cups Panko bread crumbs (or stale, crustless bread, minced)
- ¼ cup minced, flat parsley
- ¼ cup grated Romano cheese
- 2 tbsps. olive oil
- 1 tsp. garlic powder
- salt and black pepper
- 2 cups marinara sauce

Thanks to the popularity of fried calamari rings, the lowly squid is not only easier to find in the supermarket, but also a little less alien to the general population. This is another Christmas Eve essential in our family, enthusiastically awaited… by some.

PREPARATION

- Starting with cleaned squid will save you time, though the cleaning process isn't difficult: pull (or snip) the heads off the tubes. Reach a finger in the tube to clean it out, making sure to remove the translucent cuttlebone. Peel off the skin. Clean the tentacles, first cutting off anything that may still be attached and then popping out the beak which is centrally located at the base of the tentacle ring. Rinse cleaned squid thoroughly.
- The tentacles can be minced, sautéed for 5 minutes with a little olive oil, and added to the stuffing. If your guests are the braver sort, add the whole tentacles to the marinara sauce and let them cook while you stuff the tubes. I like to toss them in some seasoned flour and fry them up as an appetizer, adding some rings made from any small or broken "tubes".
- In a mixing bowl, combine bread crumbs, parsley, cheese, garlic powder, black pepper, and olive oil. Stuff tubes about ½ full (or they will split while baking). The easiest way I've found is using a big funnel and a chopstick! Close the tube with a toothpick.
- Coat the bottom of a baking dish with some of the marinara sauce; add the calamari, then top with the remaining sauce. Bake in 350° F oven for 30 minutes.

Wine Pairing

A medium bodied, fruity red wine with moderate acidity such as a Tempranillo.
SUGGESTION: Marques de Caro Tempranillo from Valencia, Spain.

Zucchini Creole a la Rene

PREP TIME: 25 MINUTES **COOK TIME: 15 MINUTES** **TOTAL: 40 MINUTES** **SERVES 4–6**

INGREDIENTS

- 2 cups diced zucchini
- 2 large tomatoes peeled & chopped or 1 8 oz. can
- 2 celery stalks and leaves, diced
- 1 medium green pepper, diced
- 1 large onion, diced
- 1½ tsp. rice
- ⅛ tsp. poultry seasoning
- ⅛ tsp. garlic salt
- dash nutmeg
- dash basil
- dash Worcestershire
- salt and pepper to taste

My mother made this an extra special dish by using many vegetables from her and my father's garden.

PREPARATION

- Mix all ingredients in a large skillet and simmer over low heat for 15 minutes or until vegetables are tender.
- Serve over white or brown rice and sprinkle soy sauce on top.

Wine Pairing

A medium bodied red that is bright with minerals such as a Zweigelt from Austria.

SUGGESTION: Nittnaus Zweigelt Vom Heideboden from Burgenland, Austria.

Geneva Gorgo

Twenty people for Thanksgiving? No problem. Christmas Eve dinner for two dozen, followed by breakfast for the survivors? Of course! Why else would a family of four own two stoves and two refrigerators.

My brother and I (sitting on Gram's lap) came from a long line of good cooks and strong women. The older I get, the better the memories.

Celebrating one of many holiday dinners with Aunt Flo, my mom, Genevieve, me (Geneva) and my brother Bill.

Hi. My name is Bill Gorgo. You may remember me from such recipes as Breaded Cauliflower and Pastina with Egg. My sister's name is Geneva—accent on the first syllable, please—and this is her story. I'm writing it so she'll get herself a dog.

Okay, so maybe your family's dealings aren't as convoluted as ours. Good for you. Keep it simple. We're not all so lucky.

Geneva has spent the last six months wrestling with some serious health issues, including six weeks when many doctors were convinced she had cancer. In the thick of it, she published a journal of her experiences for her friends and relatives via the wonderful website CaringBridge.org. Now you'd think a woman so together that she could share her pain, her struggles, and her fears could write a few measly paragraphs about making pizza dough, wouldn't you? Nope. After much begging on her part, I finally offered her this: I'd write her story for her if she'd get herself a dog. I think she'll take the deal; I know how much she doesn't want to write about her cooking career!

The fact is, Geneva has cooking issues. My mother was, in her way, as intimidating a presence in the kitchen as my father was under the hood of a motor vehicle. They both excelled in their areas of expertise, and the bars—real or perceived—were set high for those of us expected to follow in their footsteps. As a teacher, I know how quickly impossible expectations can kill any desire to learn. Eventually, Geneva fled the pressures of the kitchen as surely as I did from the garage, which is not to say she can't cook and I can't do basic car maintenance. It's just that there are... limitations.

In her case, the limitation has to do with company. Check out her recipes; the woman can make some wonderful dishes. But understand this: Mom's strength was putting on the big bash. Twenty people for Thanksgiving? No problem. Christmas Eve dinner for two dozen, followed by breakfast for the survivors and Christmas Dinner for a score of in-laws? Of course! Why else would a family of four own two stoves and two refrigerators? Just hand Mom her apron and then go hide, preferably with the neighbors.

If there isn't food for double the number of guests, there just isn't enough! Everyone brought a special dish for my mom's (head of table) 80th birthday.

As a result, Geneva (who enjoys food as much as anyone I know and enjoys the company of others at her table more than most) never learned the skills, the art, or the joy of making it all happen. Planning the menu, doing the shopping and prep work, figuring out the cooking logistics so that all the dishes are ready when they're supposed to be—this is what Geneva believes cooking is all about, namely all the things she thinks she was supposed to learn and didn't. Guilt—the quintessential Italian apéritif.

She's wrong, of course; otherwise, the men who staff military kitchens would be considered the greatest chefs ever. In fact, the cooks in the service do an amazing job under extraordinarily difficult circumstances, but let's face it— no one's enlisting for the cuisine. Cooking is about the care and love one puts into the preparation of food, whether one dish or fifty, whether feeding an army or fixing a midnight snack. That's why we remember with such affection Aunt Marie's *kolachky* and Aunt Flo's fudge, Nunz's *melanzane* and Lillian Indrebo's Christmas cookies, and all the wonderful dishes made and served to us with love throughout our lives.

Geneva is a terrific cook and an even better writer, but I'm glad she made me write this story for her. I really think she's going to enjoy having her very own dog.

If stressed spelled backwards is desserts, why not start with this course first after a long hard day?

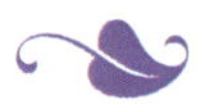

Marilyn Aleide

7

Desserts

Almond Crescent Cookies

PREP TIME: 30 MINUTES COOK TIME: 20 MINUTES TOTAL: 50 MINUTES YIELDS 25 MEDIUM COOKIES

INGREDIENTS

- ½ pound stick salted butter
- 2 cups all-purpose flour
- 5 oz. finely ground almonds
- 5 tbsps. sugar
- 2 tsps. vanilla
- ½ tsp. salt
- 1 tbsp. water
- 2 cups powdered sugar
- 2 large, flat cookie sheets

The secret ingredient to soft buttery tasting crescent almond powder sugar cookies is the amount of finely ground almonds you add and not the butter.

PREPARATION

- Cream butter and then add in sugar, powdered sugar, vanilla, and water. Mix with a whisk.
- Sift flour and salt together. Mix this in slowly. The flour will now start to turn the liquid substance into dough. You will now start to mix this by hand as it starts to thicken.
- Slowly add in the finely ground almonds. This mixture will continue to thicken and will require kneading the contents by hand to ensure the finely ground nuts are thoroughly mixed throughout.
- Pull some dough apart, approximately two or more tablespoons worth, roll this out like a short stick, then form a crescent shape and place on a cookie sheet.
- Heat oven to 325° F and bake for approximately 20 minutes.
- Remove cookie sheet from oven and let stand to warm, not cool. Roll each lukewarm crescent in powder sugar and set aside. Repeat this process until all of the crescents have been coated with powder sugar.

Wine Pairing

A light bodied, slightly sparkling, medium to sweet, low alcohol, refreshing white with stone fruit notes such as a Moscato.

SUGGESTION: Angioletta Moscato from Puglia, Italy.

Aunt Irene's Czech Cookies

PREP TIME: 20 MINUTES SERVES 8–10

INGREDIENTS

- ½ pound butter
- 1 cup sugar
- 2 egg yolks
- 1½ tsps. vanilla extract
- 2 cups flour
- 1 cup preserves of your choice
- 1 cup chopped nuts

This is a simple and delicious cookie recipe given to me by my aunt, who was an excellent cook and baker.

PREPARATION

- Cream butter; add sugar until light and fluffy.
- Add egg yolks and mix well.
- Fold in nuts.
- Spoon ½ of batter onto a greased cookie sheet and roll it with a floured roller toward the ends of the cookie sheet until bottom is completely covered with cookie dough.
- Spread preserves completely across the top of the dough. Drop remaining dough on top of the preserves.
- Bake at 325° F in a preheated oven for 45 minutes.

Wine Pairing

Crisp, clean and slightly sweet late harvest dessert wine with peach and slight grape notes and floral and spice aromas such as a Moscato. **SUGGESTION:** Field of Dreams Moscato from southeast Australia.

Brown Nut Squares

PREP TIME: 20 MINUTES COOK TIME: 20 MINUTES TOTAL: 40 MINUTES SERVES 8

INGREDIENTS

- 1 large egg
- 1 cup dark brown sugar
- ½ cup unsifted flour
- ¼ tsp. baking soda
- ¼ tsp. salt
- 1 tsp. vanilla
- 1½ cups chopped walnuts

My parents had two walnut trees in their back yard and used fresh walnuts which were amazing in this dessert!

PREPARATION

- Stir together (do not beat) egg, brown sugar, and vanilla.
- Quickly stir in flour, baking soda, vanilla, and walnuts.
- Spread into greased 8" × 8" × 2" inch pan and bake at 350° F for 20 minutes.

Wine Pairing

A delicious Riesling. **SUGGESTION:** St. Christopher Piesporter Goldtröpfchen Kabinett from Mosel, Germany. *Vintage 2010 won Silver Medal/89 pts, Beverage Tasting Institute.*

Cannoli Filling

PREP TIME: 20 MINUTES TOTAL: 20 MINUTES YIELDS 16 SHELLS

INGREDIENTS

- 32 oz. container whole milk ricotta cheese
- ¾ cup powdered sugar
- ¾ cup Mascarpone cheese
- ½ tsp. vanilla
- ½ tsp. ground cinnamon
- ⅛ tsp. salt
- 1½ cups semisweet chocolate chips
- 2 cups ground pistachio nuts, can be purchased in bags
- 20 Italian style light cannoli pastry shells, use additional for breakage
- 1 cup powdered sugar in a shaker bottle to garnish shells

Cannoli is one of the most popular Italian desserts. In Italy, they are called Cannoli Siciliani. This is a Napoli version of a Sicilian tradition.

The ricotta cheese is the main ingredient to the filling and must be drained overnight and squeezed dry to allow all of the liquid to be eliminated.

PREPARATION

- Place the ricotta cheese in a large colander and gently, but thoroughly squeeze the ricotta throughout the mixture with your hands to break it up so the water will drain through. Store overnight in the refrigerator with a cloth over the top and a pan underneath the colander to catch the remaining water.
- In a large mixing bowl, add the dry ricotta cheese, Mascarpone cheese, powdered sugar, vanilla, salt and cinnamon, and mix with a blender on low to medium until you have whipped the contents into a light and fluffy mixture.
- Add in the final ingredient, which is the semisweet chocolate chips and mix these by hand so you don't break the chips. Refrigerate bowl until contents are chilled. When ready to serve the dessert, fill a pastry bag with the filling and fill shells so the filling is completely through with excess protruding out of both ends of the shell. This will allow you to dip the ends in the garnish of chopped pistachio nuts. Sprinkle powdered sugar on shell tops and serve.

Wine Pairing

A dessert wine with a rich entry that leads to a sweet full-bodied palate with a nervy edge of acidity. **SUGGESTION:** Nittnaus Premium Trockenbeerenausles from Austria.

Carrot Cake

PREP TIME: 20 MINUTES COOK TIME: 60 MINUTES TOTAL: 80 MINUTES SERVES 6

This family favorite has been carried across the country to satisfy birthday requests. Even the next generation gives it rave reviews.

INGREDIENTS

- 2 cups sugar
- 1½ cups oil
- 4 eggs
- 2¼ cups flour
- 2 tsps. salt
- 2½ tsps. cinnamon
- 2 tsps. baking soda
- ½ tsp. nutmeg
- 1 tsp. ground cloves
- 2 cups shredded carrots
- 1½ cup walnuts (optional)
- 1 8 oz. package cream cheese, softened
- ¼ cup margarine
- 1 tsp. vanilla
- 1 pound confectioners' sugar

PREPARATION

- Heat oven to 300° F. Combine sugar, oil, eggs, and beat at medium speed for 2 minutes.
- Mix dry ingredients together, add to oil mixture, and beat at low speed for 1 minute. Add carrots and nuts.
- Spread in greased 13" × 9" pan or tube pan. Bake at 300° F for 1 hour. Test with a toothpick. Frost when cool.

PREPARATION: FROSTING

- Beat together softened cream cheese and margarine.
- Add vanilla.
- Beat in sugar gradually. If necessary, thin with milk.

Wine Pairing

A sweet white wine with fruit flavors of peach and orange like a late harvest Riesling. **SUGGESTION:** Bauer Haus Auslese from Rheinhessen, Germany. *Vintage 2009 won Silver Medal/87 pts, Beverage Tasting Institute.*

Chocolate Frosting

PREP TIME: 10 MINUTES **COOK TIME: 2 MINUTES** **TOTAL: 12 MINUTES** **YIELDS 1½ CUPS**

INGREDIENTS

- 2 squares semi-sweet chocolate
- 4 tbsps. margarine
- 2 cups powdered sugar
- 3 tbsps. milk
- 1 tsp. vanilla

Have you ever looked at a cake and wanted to drag your finger through the frosting? This is that frosting.

PREPARATION

- Melt chocolate and margarine together.
- Add powdered sugar, milk, and vanilla. Beat well.
- This is a great frosting mix for layered cakes, cupcakes, brownies and more.

Wine Pairing

With so many options of what you can top using this frosting, a wine with a delicate sweetness and harmonious acidity would be a safe choice. **SUGGESTION:** Esterházy Blaufränkisch Eiswein from Burgenland, Austria.

gorgonzola cheese
Balsamic vinegarette

Fran's Cream Cheese Pound Cake

PREP TIME: 25 MINUTES COOK TIME: 2 HOURS 15 MINUTES TOTAL: 2 HOURS 40 MINUTES SERVES 8–12

INGREDIENTS

1	8 oz. package cream cheese
1	pound butter
8	large eggs
4	cups sugar
4	cups cake flour
4	tbsps. vanilla butter and nut extract
1	tbsp. vanilla extract

This is a very rich pound cake which I have been making on a weekly basis for the past 18 years.

PREPARATION

- Blend together cream cheese and butter; mix well. Add sugar and blend well.
- Slowly add eggs, one at a time, mixing well. Add extracts. Slowly add cake flour and blend well.
- Turn out into a well-greased and floured angel food tube pan.
- Bake in preheated oven at 325° F for 2–2¼ hours or until done. Cover top loosely with foil after baking for 1½ hours and continue baking with foil for the remaining time.
- Top with your favorite glaze. I like to drizzle a powdered sugar and water mixture over the top of the cake.

Wine Pairing

A full bodied, late harvest dessert wine from overripe berries with great aromatics and a pleasant, but not offensive, sweetness such as a Beernauslese.
SUGGESTION: Schlink Haus Beerenauslese.

Irene's Polish Kuch Bread

PREP TIME: 20 MINUTES COOK/RISING TIME: 4 HOURS TOTAL: 4 HOURS 20 MINUTES YIELDS 2 (4"×9") TINS

INGREDIENTS

1 cup lukewarm milk
3 yeast packets
2 cups flour
1 tsp. salt
1 cup sugar
8 egg yolks plus
1 whole egg
1 tsp. lemon juice
1 tsp. grated lemon rind
¼ pound melted unsalted butter
3 cups flour
1½ cup golden raisins
1 beaten egg white
3 tbsp. sugar
3 tbsp. flour

This recipe takes time due to the rising involved, but it's well worth it. If you have a large ceramic bowl, use it for this recipe. Kuch is Polish sweet bread that's made for special occasions. It freezes well and is delicious toasted.

PREPARATION

- Dissolve 3 yeast packets into 1 cup lukewarm milk.
- Add 2 cups flour and beat well. Set aside in a warm place for 45 minutes.
- Add salt, sugar, and 8 egg yolks plus one whole egg and beat well.
- Add lemon rind and juice, melted butter, and 3 cups flour. Mix well and let rise until double in size.
- Add raisins and put into 2 greased 5" × 9" × 2.5" loaf pans and brush tops with slightly beaten egg white.
- Combine 3 tablespoons sugar, 3 tablespoons flour, and 1½ tablespoons butter and sprinkle on top of bread loaves.
- Let rise for 1 hour and then bake in a 350° F oven for 1 hour.
- Test with toothpick. When done remove from oven and cool for 30 minutes before removing from tin.

Wine Pairing

A tropical fruit toting, slightly sweet white wine such as a Moscato. **SUGGESTION:** Angioletta Moscato-Airen from Spain.

Mary Ann's Chocolate Zucchini Cake

PREP TIME: 15 MINUTES COOK TIME: 1 HOUR 15 MINUTES TOTAL: 1 HOUR 30 MINUTES SERVES 8–12

INGREDIENTS: CAKE

- 3 cups all-purpose flour
- 3 cups sugar
- 1¼ tsps. baking powder
- 1¼ tsps. baking soda
- ¼ tsp. cinnamon
- 1½ cups corn or vegetable oil
- 2 squares melted Baker's Chocolate
- 4 eggs
- 1½ tsps. vanilla extract
- ½ tsps. almond extract
- 3 cups grated zucchini
- 1 cup chopped nuts
- 1 cup chopped dates

INGREDIENTS: FROSTING

- 1 stick butter
- 2 cups confectioners' sugar
- 1 square Baker's Chocolate

Wine Pairing

A soft, late harvested, fruity red wine. **SUGGESTION:** Bauer Haus Sweet Red from Rheinhessen, Germany. *Vintage 2010 won Bronze Medal/82 pts, Beverage Tasting Institute.*

This recipe is contributed by my godmother, Mary Ann. She is a great cook and baker and this cake is a much anticipated dessert at our annual St. Rocco Feast Day.

PREPARATION

- Sift flour, baking powder, and cinnamon, set aside.
- Beat eggs until frothy. Beat sugar and oil, and then add cooled chocolate, vanilla, and almond extract.
- Fold in dry ingredients; fold in zucchini, nuts, and dates.
- Pour mixture into greased and floured 10-inch tube pan.
- Preheat oven to 350º F and bake of 1 hour and 15 minutes. Cool for 20 minutes. Remove from pan and let stand until completely cooled.

PREPARATION: FROSTING

- In a large bowl, beat 1 stick of butter, 1 cup of confectioner's sugar, and 1 square of Baker's Chocolate. Beat all ingredients until very smooth in order to make the icing of good spreading consistency.

Mary's Cheesecake

PREP TIME: 15 MINUTES COOK TIME: 1 HOUR 10 MINUTES TOTAL: 1 HOUR 25 MINUTES SERVES 8

INGREDIENTS

- 1 graham cracker crust
- 1 pound cream cheese, softened
- 1 cup granulated sugar
- 4 eggs, separated
- 2 tbsps. flour
- 1 cup milk
- ¼ tsp. salt
- 1 tsp. vanilla

This easy-to-make cheesecake was dessert after every Sunday meal at my in-laws. Cherry pie filling was always the topping of choice.

PREPARATION

- Heat oven to 350° F. Line an 8 inch square baking dish with a graham cracker crust.
- Beat together cream cheese, sugar, and 4 beaten egg yolks.
- Add flour, milk, salt, and vanilla.
- Fold in beaten egg whites.
- Pour into prepared baking dish.
- Bake at 350° F for 1 hour and 10 minutes.
- When cool, serve plain or topped with berries.

Wine Pairing

A nice, semi-sweet, sparkling wine would be a great pair. **SUGGESTION:** Pearly Bay Celebration from Cape Winelands, South Africa. *Won 84 pts, Wine Enthusiast.*

Nina's Lemon Pie

PREP TIME: 20 MINUTES   COOK TIME: 10 MINUTES   TOTAL: 30 MINUTES   SERVES 6–8

INGREDIENTS

- 1 cup granulated sugar, divided into two parts
- 2 tbsps. cornstarch
- 2 tbsps. flour
- 1/4 tsp. salt
- 1 lemon rind, grated
- 2 cups boiling water
- 2 eggs, separated
- 6 tbsps. lemon juice
- 1 cooked pie crust

This was my Dad's favorite dessert, and was his version of birthday cake. Sometimes Mom used it as a peace offering!

PREPARATION

- Mix cornstarch, flour, salt, lemon rind, and ½ cup sugar in a large bowl. Set aside.
- Mix ½ cup sugar, egg yolks, and lemon juice in a small bowl. In a separate bowl beat egg whites until stiff.
- Boil water and add some to large bowl. Mix until smooth. Pour large bowl contents into boiling water and cook until clear and thick. Add ¼ teaspoon of salt.
- Add small bowl to pot and cook for 2 minutes. Fold in beaten egg whites, pour into baked pie crust. Garnish and serve at room temperature after pie filling has set.

Wine Pairing

A medium bodied white wine with good minerality such as a Riesling. **SUGGESTION:** Weingut H.J. & E. Lehmen Estates, Zeller Schwarze Katz Riesling QbA, Hochgewächs Fruchtsüss. *Gold Medal BTI, 90 pts, and previous vintage, 86 pts Wine Enthusiast*

Nita's Apple Pie

PREP TIME: 45 MINUTES COOK TIME: 90 MINUTES TOTAL: 2 HOURS 15 MINUTES SERVES 6

INGREDIENTS

10	large Granny Smith apples
1	large sweet pear
⅓	cup light brown sugar
1	cup white sugar
¼	tsp. salt
½	stick salted butter
½	stick salted butter for pats
1	tsp. nutmeg
1	tsp. vanilla
1	tsp. cinnamon
1	package refrigerated pre-rolled pie crust

This recipe has an honored place in the dessert section. It was given to me my dear friend Nita who taught me the techniques of country-style cooking and who gave me the secret ingredient to the apple pie.

PREPARATION

- In a large bowl, peel and cut the apples and the pear into medium size slices.
- In a separate mixing bowl, fold in brown sugar, white sugar, softened butter, salt, nutmeg, vanilla, and cinnamon and whisk thoroughly. Then pour this mixture into the first bowl and mix thoroughly with your hands until all of the slices are coated.
- Remove the two pre-packaged pie crust discs and take one of the discs and form the bottom crust into a 9 inch pie pan making sure the edges overlap the ring edge of the pie pan.
- Pour mixture into the pie crust bottom, which will form a high mound. Add small pats of butter throughout, approximately 8. Then take the second pie crust disc and with a rolling pin, roll the edges to expand the circumference of the circle about an inch and a half. Cover the mound completely and press the edges together to meet the overlap dough from the bottom crust. Use your fingers and thumb and twist the edges to form the crust of the pie all around.
- Use a knife to cut slits in the top of the crust. This will help the air flow and heat to cook the pie inside and make a nice design when baked to a golden brown. Heat at 365° F for 90 minutes.
- Secret ingredient: the pear.

Wine Pairing

A sweet, white wine such as a late harvest Riesling. **SUGGESTION:** St. Christopher Piesporter Goldtröpfchen Auslese from the Mosel region of Germany.

Pizzelles

PREP TIME: 15 MINUTES **COOK TIME: 70 MINUTES** **TOTAL: 1 HOUR 25 MINUTES** **YIELDS 90–100**

INGREDIENTS

6 large eggs
1½ cups sugar
2 sticks margarine, melted
1 tsp. vanilla
2 tsps. anise extract
3½ cups flour, sifted
4 tsps. baking powder
pinch of salt

You will need a pizzelle iron to make these special cookies. I have a Prego Pizzelle Maker, but a variety of irons are available.

PREPARATION

- Heat the pizzelle iron according to the manufacturer's directions and spray lightly with cooking spray.
- Beat eggs, sugar, margarine, vanilla, and anise together well.
- Gradually add sifted flour, baking powder, and salt to egg mixture using the lowest electric beater setting. The batter should be soft enough to be dropped by a spoon.
- Drop a teaspoon of batter into center of each preheated grid pattern.
- Close lid and bake approximately 30–40 seconds depending on your preference for browning and/or the consistency of your batter. Be alert!
- Lift the lid and remove cooked pizzelles with the edge of a fork. Place them on aluminum foil lined cooling racks in single layers. When they are completely cool, you may stack them. When serving, sprinkle each pizzelle with powdered sugar.
- Store pizzelles only in cookie cans; plastic containers will make the cookies soft. Store in the refrigerator or a cool place.

Wine Pairing

A bright, fresh, crisp acidic, sparkling white wine with supple fruit such as a Prosecco. **SUGGESTION:** Zuccotti Prosecco from Veneto, Italy.

Roz's Blueberry Muffins

PREP TIME: 15 MINUTES COOK TIME: 15–20 MINUTES TOTAL: 35 MINUTES SERVES 12

INGREDIENTS

- 2 cups sifted flour
- ½ cup sugar
- 1 tbsp. baking powder
- ½ tsp. salt
- 2 eggs, beaten
- ½ cup oil
- ½ cup milk
- ½ pint blueberries, washed
- ½ stick butter, melted
- sugar (to dip muffins into)

These have to be the best blueberry muffins I have ever had. They are so easy to put together and very moist; the sugar and butter topping—delicious.

PREPARATION

- Heat oven to 400° F. Grease muffin cups or line with muffin liners. Sift flour with sugar, baking powder, and salt into mixing bowl.
- Combine eggs, oil, and milk.
- Make a well in the center of dry ingredients. Add liquid ingredients all at once; mix only until all dry particles are moist. Fold in blueberries.
- Fill paper lined muffin cups evenly (about ¾ full). Bake at 400° F for 15–20 minutes until toothpick comes out clean.
- Dip muffin tops in melted butter, then in sugar.

Wine Pairing

A full bodied, late harvest sweet white wine such as an Auslese. **SUGGESTION:** Bauer Haus Auslese from Rheinhessen, Germany. *Vintage 2009 won Silver Medal/87 pts, Beverage Tasting Institute.*

Sam's Biscotti

PREP TIME: 20 MINUTES **COOK TIME: 30 MINUTES** **TOTAL: 50 MINUTES**

INGREDIENTS

- 1½ sticks margarine, softened
- 1 cup sugar
- 1 tsp. anise or orange flavoring
- 2 eggs
- 2 cups flour
- 1 tsp. baking soda
- 1 tsp. baking powder
- 2 big tbsps. sour cream
- 2 additional cups flour

Every time I went to my mother-in-law's home there was a tin of biscotti on the table. Even though they disappear quickly, they could last for weeks.

PREPARATION

- Heat oven to 350° F.
- Mix together margarine, sugar, flavoring, and eggs until well blended.
- Combine flour, baking soda, and baking powder.
- Alternately add the flour mixture and two big spoons of sour cream to the margarine mixture beginning and ending with the flour mixture.
- Add the additional flour and blend until dough forms.
- Divide dough into 5 logs about 1 inch round and 6-inch long and place on a greased cookie sheet. Bake at 350° F about 20 minutes.
- Remove from oven and let rest a few minutes. Cut into slices and place cut side down on cookie sheet and return to oven for 5 minutes. Turn over again to other side and bake another 5 minutes. Store in tin container lined with wax paper.

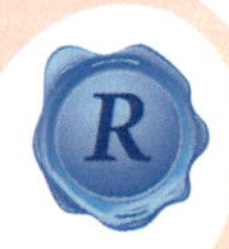

Wine Pairing

A refreshing, subtle, slight sweet, sparkling white wine such as a Moscato.
SUGGESTION: Gelisi Antonio Moscato Dolce. *Rated an "Exceptional Best Buy" by the Beverage Tasting Institute.*

Tiramisu

PREP TIME: 15 MINUTES   COOK TIME: 1 HOUR   TOTAL: 1 HOUR 15 MINUTES   SERVES 4–6

INGREDIENTS

- 3 egg yolks
- ¼ cup white sugar
- 2 tsps. vanilla
- 1 ⅛ cups Mascarpone cheese
- 2 tbsps. unsweetened cocoa powder
- 24 lady fingers
- 4 cups brewed black Espresso coffee

INGREDIENTS: OPTIONAL

- 2 oz. Cognac or Brandy

A favorite dessert from Venice, Italy, Tiramisu means "pick-me-up" and is most popular in chic Italian restaurants and homes. This is a simple version that has a great gourmet taste.

PREPARATION

- In a medium bowl, beat egg yolks and mix in sugar and vanilla until smooth and light yellow in color. Fold in the Mascarpone and stir. Set aside. Add Cognac or Brandy (optional).
- Brew a pot of Espresso coffee. Dip 12 lady fingers briefly in the coffee, but do not soak them. Arrange lady fingers in a row on the bottom of an 8" × 8" glass or ceramic pan.
- Spread half of the Mascarpone mixture evenly over the lady fingers creating a layer of filling. Sprinkle the cocoa powder over the surface.
- Add a second row of dipped lady fingers in the same manner across the pan creating another layer. Follow up with pouring on the other half of the Mascarpone mixture to cover the surface. Sprinkle with the cocoa powder over the complete surface. Cover and chill in the refrigerator for one hour.
- Add a dollop of Mascarpone on the top. With a fork, whisk through the dollop to make a grooved pattern, than sprinkle more cocoa over it to color. It's ready to serve.

Wine Pairing

A sweet, semi-sparkling white wine such as a Moscato d'Asti.
SUGGESTION: Lonati Moscato d'Asti.

Marilyn Aleide

All my children love to cook, bake and entertain, and they have passed this on to their children. Their cooking questions assure me that the time spent all of those years preparing the meals continues to be a way for them to connect to their roots.

Dinner was never complete without demi-tasse coffee served with love by my mother, Nina. That's me on the left learning the art of hospitality from the best.

Never too young to learn how to make meatballs! Granddaughters, Emma and Nina, never knew what "fun" awaited them at grandma's house.

"Eat to live?" or "Live to eat?" Growing up in an Italian family in the Bronx, the meal was the major focus of family life. Of course, the fact that my father was a butcher had something to do with that. "I can't give you much, but I will always put food on the table" was a promise he was able to keep for many years. From the finest meats at the market to the freshest fish caught on his day off, from the wildest mushrooms found in the woods to zucchini flowers from the garden and carduna found along the side of the road, his time was spent planning the meals my mother would artfully prepare and serve.

Every night we waited for my dad to come home from the butcher shop before we sat down all together to have our evening meal. This was not an option; it was not an order; this is just what we did and we truly believed that this was what life was about – coming together at the end of the day to share the food and the day with those we loved.

Appetizers and desserts were not part of the meal—except on holidays—but Aunt Bessie was the baker in the family and our sweet tooths were nourished by her creations. We loved her and her desserts and looked forward to those special times we could splurge. None of us had a lot of "stuff", but we had a love of fresh, well-prepared food, shared with family and friends.

I can't say that I grew up cooking, other than an occasional marinara sauce; there were too many others around to prepare the meals. It was only after I was married that the kitchen became my domain and the responsibility to gather others became one of the joys in my life. Now there was not just a mother, aunt and grandmother to pass on recipes but there was also a mother-in-law who showed me how to make pizza fritta, meatballs, and cheesecake.

Spending summers on Cape Cod inspired me to learn to shuck clams and stuff lobsters, while friends from Paris and Greece taught me how to make the lightest flourless chocolate cake and the most savory spanikopita. As a stay-at-home mom raising four children, cooking became my creative outlet and they became my taste-testers. The challenge of stretching a chicken into four different meals during leaner times to finding new ways to cook the overabundant crop of zucchini from the garden were welcome distractions from everyday duties.

My father, Mario the butcher, at the head of the table, was happiest surrounded by all his children and grandchildren, sharing Sunday dinner. Aunt Bessie and Uncle John completed the picture.

Not surprisingly, all my children love to cook and bake and entertain, and they have passed this on to their children. A call from one of them asking how to make a certain dish assures me that the time spent all those years preparing meals and gathering family and friends to share our table continues to be a way for them to connect with their roots and make present the love of so many over the years. Now that my children are cooking for their families and friends, I find myself calling them for new recipes when I need a little change in the menu. The teacher has become the student—it's a wonderful thing!

I would not have chosen any other way to come to adulthood other than the way I did—with a love of fresh food, prepared lovingly and served to those who looked forward to sitting around a simple table at the end of the day. As this was my legacy from my parents, I hope I have passed this on to my children and grandchildren—and now to you!

Our success lies in our ability to study the market to spot trends and to select what's new and different in the marketplace of today and to predict future trends from around the world.

Manfred Bauer, Wein-Bauer, Inc

8

Wine & Beer

HAUS
Kabinett Nahe
PRÄDIKATSWEIN
KABINETT

Introduction

I am Manfred Bauer, owner and CEO of Wein-Bauer, Inc As a premier importer of great wines, spirits and beers from around the world; we create and market some of the most innovative and exciting labels to hit the U.S. today. Our rapid growth in this country and abroad is by design, and we have strategically developed our niche market, through careful consideration, extensive knowledge with global markets and our expertise gained from the family business spanning several generations.

I spent most of my childhood and early years working in my father's winery in Stockerau, Austria learning my craft and developing the Wein-Bauer brand before I relocated to the United States with my wife, Gaby to expand the international initiatives to U.S. In 1980, we launched Wein-Bauer, Inc. in Franklin Park, Illinois, a suburb just west of Chicago.

As a Chicago-based and family-run operation, with well over 30 years of experience to date, we developed a niche in the market by offering a unique selection of wines, spirits and select beers coupled with "special finds", of which many of these selections are otherwise not available outside of their native regions or countries.

Our success lies in our ability to study the market to spot trends and to select what's new and different in the marketplace of today and to predict future trends from around the world, with special attention to, Austria, Germany, Italy and Spain.

Our history is enriched with the family tradition of wine making and dates back to several generations. I am the grandson of the legendary Austrian vintner family founder, Leopold Bauer, and son of Otto Sr. Bauer. This father and son team originally made their mark in the wine industry in 1932 in Stockerau, Austria, where for many generations they produced hundreds of award-winning and nationally recognized wines. Their winery was one of the first to bring prized Rieslings and other varietals to the international import/export marketplace as well as becoming a pioneer of Austrian wine in the U.S.

Today, Wein-Bauer, has an extensive product offering from Austria, Germany, Italy and Spain and many other countries and regions from around the globe. Our goal is to introduce you to new sights, smells and tastes with the recommendations we have made. We know our brands intimately well, and the passion behind the wine maker and the vineyards that yield them, making these introductions all the more special. And, we have added a number of award-winning selections throughout the book that I am sure you will enjoy.

In *Life Beyond Takeout!* we have recommended varietals and/or paired specific labels for each recipe that will enhance your culinary experience and take your meal planning to a new level.

This varied collection of recipes truly goes beyond the dish and exemplifies family traditions that embrace a variety of experiences and culinary tastes from each of the chefs who have submitted them. From comfort foods to gourmet celebrations you will find that our recommendations are the "perfect" match to each of the appetizers, soups, salads, sides, pastas, main dishes and desserts that you will encounter.

In the following pages you can expect to find some basic guidelines on the pairing process. As you will see there are no *formal* rules that apply, and your personal preference will ultimately rule the day when selecting a wine or craft beer with each meal.

The pairings we made throughout the book include some "medal" winners and "rated" labels that you may want to take special note of. You can find this list on page 234.

In addition, we have added a comprehensive list of all the pairing suggestions organized by *food group* and *recipe page* to make it easier for you to look up pairing options until you become more familiar with the label names.

Our goal here is two-fold in that we want to educate and guide you through the pairing process, but more importantly, we want to take you *beyond* the label into a world of antiquity and tradition. Our relationships with each of these brands extend well beyond the "bottle", as these brands mirror the same family traditions of the many vintners that produce them.

For this reason, we have profiled one Austrian winery, one German winery, and one Italian brewery so that you can come to know the family traditions and the passion beyond some of our labels. Each has their own history, personality, recipes and blends, and this is translated into the embodiment of their superb and unique taste.

We want you to experience the journey with every sip. We want your next meal to be more than just "food and drink" but a truly memorable experience when breaking bread with your family and friends.

A perfect match. *Bon Appetit!*
Viel Freude beim Essen und Trinken. Guten Appetit!

Manfred Bauer, Owner/CEO

Turn Me Red
ESTERHÁZY
AUSTRIA
HAYDN
MERLOT
2007
BAUER HAUS AUSLESE
2009 RHEINHESSEN
PRÄDIKATSWEIN
WHITE WINE
BRONZENE KAMMERPREISMÜNZE
LANDESPRÄMIERUNG
WEINGUT-PENSION H.J.&E. LEHMEN
D-56856 ZELL-KAIMT/MOSEL · TEL. 0 65 42 / 46 28
HOCHGEWÄCHS
TROCKEN
BEER FROM ITALY
COLLESI
BEER FROM ITALY
COLLESI

Wine Pairing Notes

As you may have noticed each of the recipes in this book comes with a pairing suggestion, compliments of your friends at Wein-Bauer. We just thought, "What better way to make that delicious meal even *more* delicious?", and our answer…of course is wine, or in some cases a hand crafted beer.

With there being so many options out there, and virtually no rules apply, yes, I did say *no* rules, we encourage you to take a leap of faith with some or your own ideas as well, after you have read some of our helpful pairing notes. The most exciting part of pairing food with a variety of wines and beers will ultimately come down to your personal preference anyway, so isn't that what really matters?

Wine connoisseurs make wine drinking seem so complicated. With all due respect to their expertise in determining fine wine through the use of their basic senses of sight and smell during a "tasting", these individuals hold out their arms and swirl the wine in their glasses, evaluating subtle nuances in a wine's color giving clues to its variety, region, and age, and then they stick their noses deep into their glasses sniffing the aromas to determine what grapes were used, or where they were grown or how they were fermented. The final test is the "taste" in which they use words like "depth" and "nose" or "long" and "earthy".

On the most basic level, however, enjoying wine and hand crafted beers relies on one factor alone, and that is whether or not it tastes good to you.

2010
Riesling
Spätlese

Wine Pairing Notes

Before you hit the ground running take a moment and read over our pairing notes. This short guide and helpful hints, rules of thumb, food for thought, call it what you'd like will guide you in selecting a wine or beer compatible with the many food groups and tastes you'll find in *Life Beyond Takeout!*

WHAT TO CONSIDER WHEN CHOOSING A PAIRING?

CONTRAST

The objective when pairing wines with various foods is to join the two together so they complement one another, bringing out the best by "mirroring" or "contrasting" the flavors and creating a harmonious partnership, and remembering not to overwhelm one with the other.

WEIGHT

A great starting point for this "perfect-pairing process" is to determine the "weight" of the dish, and accompany it with a wine of equal "weight". For instance, if the dish is fairly light—seafood, salads, or mainly vegetables—your best bet is to go with a fairly light wine to keep balance. A crisp and acidic Riesling, Grüner Veltliner or Sauvignon Blanc will pair nicely with a fish or poultry dish in a creamy sauce.

The acidity will help to cut through the creaminess of the sauce and be nicely refreshing. An oaked Chardonnay just wouldn't give it that extra kick. A heavy wine, like a Cabernet Sauvignon for example, would be too powerful and simply overwhelm the lighter, delicate food.

On the other hand, if you have a fairly heavy wine, that would be a great partner for a heavier meal, like red meat dishes, since it can stand up to those bold and robust flavors typically found in steaks, chops or lamb.

Let's not forget spicy dishes! These go very well with sweeter wines using the "contrasting" method of pairing flavors. One easy indicator to determine the "weight" of the wine, either heavy or light, is the alcohol content. The higher the alcohol content, the more likely it is that the wine is heavier. Judging and understanding the balancing act will surely make choosing that much easier.

AGING CONDITIONS

Another factor to consider is how the wine is aged. Was it aged in oak barrels, and for how long, or was it aged in stainless steel? A wine aged in oak tends to be heavier than one aged in stainless steel, and the longer in oak the heavier it can become.

TASTING ORDER

It is thought best to taste/drink wine in an order of white to red, light to heavy, and drier to sweeter to ensure your palate does not become compromised. Starting out with something such as a light, white Pinot Grigio, then to an oaked Chardonnay or Pinot Noir, moving on to a heavier, red Syrah, and finishing with a late harvest or dessert wine would be the suggested progression.

PAIRING BY COURSE

APPETIZERS & FIRST COURSES

Typically, it is best to go with a lighter bodied wine for the beginning, or starter courses of a meal. The appetizer course, by definition, is meant to simply stimulate an appetite; therefore the portions are usually smaller and quicker to eat, and the ingredients and preparation methods are lighter. This course lends itself toward wines that are easy to drink, with, or without food, not too high in alcohol content, and are lower in tannins.

Grape varieties/wines to consider, but not limited to, are:

- *Sparkling* (semi to extra dry): Champagne, Proseccos, Sekts, Cava
- *Whites:* Grüner Veltliner, Riesling, Verdicchio, Vermentino, Pinot Grigio, Sauvignon Blanc, Chenin Blanc
- *Light Reds:* Pinot Noir, Red Burgundy, Beaujolais, Zweigelt, Dornfelder, Tempranillo, Sangiovese, Nebbiolo

MIDDLE & MAIN COURSES

These courses will be the ones with richer, heavier, full flavored foods, therefore would be best paired with wines that match their profile. This would be the time to introduce those medium-full bodied wines (usually reds) with higher tannins, maybe higher in alcohol, capable of standing up to, as well as complimenting, the foods being served. In some cases the appropriate wines are ones that show their true colors when joined by foods.

Grape varieties/wines to consider, but not limited to, are:

- *Whites:* Chardonnay (oaked), Gewurtztraminer, Viogner, White Burgundy
- *Reds:* Cabernet Sauvignon, Malbec, Carmenere, Zinfandel, Crianza, Merlot, Chianti, Barbera d'Alba, Barolo, Brunello, Shiraz/Syrah, Blaufränkisch

DESSERTS

Ahhh! Desserts, the end of the meal, but most certainly not the end of the fun. Am I right? After all, "stressed" is "desserts" spelled backwards and it's this comforting taste that seems to make everything ok.

So put away that tea and coffee and give yourself a real treat… some wine. For these sweet indulgences pick up a bottle that references "late harvested", or bottles that say things like "late harvest", Auslese, Beerenauslese, Trockenbeerenauslese, or Eiswein— all these are good choices.

Oh, and don't forget, Ports! Port wines are a great companion for your darker colored, richer desserts containing things like chocolate and caramel. A helpful hint is to consider the color of the wine and the color of the dessert. White wines with light colored desserts and red wines with dark colored desserts.

Beer Pairing Notes

If you're feeling froggy and up for a change, or perhaps your guests would like to explore other tastes, go for a delicious, hand crafted, high-end, micro-brewed beer.

These beers are produced with just as much craftsmanship, time and attention, and high quality ingredients as you expect from your wines, and for that reason they are definitely very food friendly.

For centuries, beer and food have been paired together, because beer offers a broad range of flavors, aromas and textures, which make it a perfect match for nearly any kind of food, from traditional sausages, pizza and hamburgers to the most luxurious dishes.

For great food pairing there are a number of factors to consider that are similar to wine pairing:

Match strength with strength, in selecting a delicate beer for a delicate dish, or strong flavored foods with a more assertive beer.

Look for *harmony and balance* with certain beer and food combinations by simply finding the right common flavor or aromas they may have in common. For example, the nutty flavor of an English-style brown ale and a Cheddar cheese burger, or the deep roasted flavor of imperial stout, and chocolate truffles or the rich caramel flavors of an Oktoberfest Lager with roasted pork are some good examples. Traditional pairing such as Schnitzel with pale lager may be obvious, but would you have thought to put stout together with oysters?

Sweetness, bitterness, carbonation, heat (spice) and richness are additional factors to consider when pairing with food's ingredients. Sounds complicated, but it's really quite straightforward.

It's all about *contrast* and *complement*. Beer and food pairings should take into consideration both, even if some pairings are more dependent on one or the other.

There are four main ingredients in craft beer; malted barley (or malted wheat or other grains), hops, yeast and water. Malt and hop flavors tend to be the most prominent and easily paired with food.

MALT

The sweetness of malt reduces the heat of spicy food. Try malty brown ale with a spicy Thai dish or a Scotch Ale with spicy Mexican food. In short, the right complement of a craft beer can diminish the heat factor.

For fired up foods, consider Brown Ale, Bocks, Porters, Red Ales, Scotch and Scottish Ales, Stouts, Vienna Lagers. Malt bonus: the flavors of malt (caramel, chocolate, graham cracker, roast, toasted, toffee) harmonize with grilled, roasted and smoked foods, because malt contains many of these flavors.

HOPS

Rich sauces have added fats and butter. Hop bitterness cuts through the fat in food and lessens the dense heavy feeling in your month. Hops' balance malt's sweetness and is the heart and soul in most craft beers.

CARBONATION

Beer's carbonation (bubbles) scrubs the tongue clean of fat and prepares you for that next bite.

You want to pair food with craft beer to the preparation of the dish instead of pairing to the original protein. Of course all flavors in any dish are determined by the preparation and its ingredients, so before you attempt to create the "perfect" pairing, ask yourself how the dish is going to be cooked? Will it be caramelized from grilling, steamed on a stove top or just tossed with olive oil? What seasonings are used? All of these factors influence the flavor of any dish from appetizers, soups, salads, sides, main fair and desserts, there is a craft beer to match for any occasion.

A perfect example of a great brand that offers a variety of options or tastes is Birra Collesi Imperale, otherwise known as just Collesi. There are six different styles of these Belgium style brewed beers created in Italy, each of which has a very different taste profile than the other. The varied flavors and tastes speak to a broad range of pairing options you can consider.

Think beef for your next meal and follow these useful, yet simple tips

Profiles

Family, Tradition & Passion

Esterházy Estates

PROFILE OF AN AUSTRIAN WINERY

Wine and winegrowing have played a central role in the life of the Esterházy Family for centuries. The cellars of the Castle of Eisenstadt already in the 17th century boasted princely vintages at the time when the Italian architect Carleone converted the castle into an early-baroque palace from 1663 to 1672 at the behest of Prince Paul I.

It was Countess Maria Lunati-Visconti, the wife of Prince Paul II Anton Esterházy (1711-1762), who instructed the princely administrator, Count Herbeviller, to import Pinot Noir vines from Burgundy and plant them in the princely vineyards.The specialties of the House of Esterházy which were cultivated from the very beginning included noble—sweet wines like high-class Spatleses and precious Trockenbeerenausleses, which can be traced back to the early 18th century. These wines were highly appreciated at the Imperial Court in Vienna.

Over the years, the offerings of the House won other famous admirers. Among them was Joseph Haydin (1732–1809), who acted for almost 30 years as the court Capellmeister (conductor) and whose creative work was largely sponsored by the princes. He actually loved the wines so much that he preferred to take a portion of his salary in the form of wine.

ESTERHÁZY

AUSTRIA

Esterházy Estates

PROFILE OF AN AUSTRIAN WINERY

Some of the excellent vineyards from that glorious time have ranked among the family's top sites til today. For instance, the single vineyard "Schneiderteil", a steep southeasterly exposed slope on the Leithaberg in St. Georgen, in the winegrowing district of Neusiedlersee-Hugelland. This exceptional vineyard was acquired by the Esterházy Family in 1778 after the dissolution of the Order of the Jesuits and is now one of the viticultural treasures of the House.

For 350 years, the traditional winery of the Esterházy Family was housed in the Meierhof in Donnerskirchen before being moved to the historic cellars of the Esterházy Palace in Eisenstadt in 1947. Yet, the limited facilities in the heritage protected vaults and the continuously growing demand for top-quality wines called for a new solution. A new, ultramodern winery for state-of-the-art vinification was established. The new winery was inaugurated with the 2006 crush. It is located in Trausdorf, not far from Eisenstadt and in eye contact to Esterházy Palace.

Esterházy Winery holds 65 hectares of vineyards in the heart of the winegrowing district Neusiedlersee-Hugelland around Eisenstadt, the capital of Burgenland. It has some of the best sites of the whole region. These are located on the southern slopes of the Leithagebirge, on the hills of the Ruster Hugelland and on the Follig mountain near GroBhoflein. The unique symbiosis between calciferous soils and the exceptional, almost Mediteranean climate, which is influenced by nearby Lake Neusiedl and the Pannonian Plain, produces wines of distinct terroir character.

A great wine tradition, ultramodern winery, fascinating portfolio of premium vineyard sites ... a dream for every winemaker. Thus, the Esterházy Family managed to win over one of Austria's best enologists, Josef Pusch, as the chief winemaker. But there is another wine luminary in whom the Esterházys aroused enthusiasm about the winery: Stephane Derenoncourt. The French enologist works as a consultant for a number of top-class chateaux in Bordeaux (e.g., Pavie-Macquin, Canon-la-Gaffeliere, La Mondotte, Smith Haut Lafitte, Prieure-Lichine), also for the California wine estate of Francis Ford Coppola, and since June of 2009, for the Esterházy Winery.

The history and family traditions live on through the estate and the wines they produce. Esterházy wines have earned numerous awards and prizes at major national and international wine competitions with gold medals and 90 point ratings as the norm.

Weingut H.J. & E. Lehmen Estates

PROFILE OF A GERMAN WINERY

Weingut H. J. & E. Lehmen Estates is a boutique estate with 3 hectares of steep hill slate vineyards. The wines are grown in the romantic town of Zell (Mosel), the wine city of the famous "Zeller Schwarze Katz" (The Black Cat) in the middle of a 2000 year old countryside in the heart of the mid-Moselle valley in Germany.

The Mosel is one of the oldest wine-growing regions in Germany. It's thought that vines were originally brought here by the Romans 2,000 years ago .

Zell, is a tiny, historic wine-making settlement located alongside the Mosel River. It's made up of many towns and villages commonly referenced as "The Zeller Land" and it's characterized by history, customs and tradition representing the center of the Mosel's wine culture. Zell can be traced back to the Roman Empire in AD 70, and later in 1222, when it was officially granted town rights. In 1794, Zell was French owned as the Rhine's left bank was occupied by French Revolutionary troops. In 1814, it was assigned to the Kingdom of Prussia at the Congress of Vienna. In the following years fires broke out in 1848 and again in 1857 which destroyed a great deal of the Old Town. Since 1946, the town has been part of the newly founded state of Rhineland-Palatinate.

The Lehmen family descendents are of celtic roman heritage, and their history dates back to 1777, when Josef Lehmen founded the winery in Zell (Mosel). Today, Herman Josef Lehmen carries on the tradition of his father, Edmund Josef Lehmen, along with his son, Jorg Josef Lehmen, and his wife Edeltraud making wine and running the estate. Herman Josef Lehmen's brother and his son team also have a winery in this region expanding the Lehmen legacy. The younger son, Tobias Lehmen, is a regional sales manager and German wine expert in the United States.

Pension
HAUS
EDELTRAUD

Weingut H.J. & E. Lehmen Estates

PROFILE OF A GERMAN WINERY

In the German town of Zell an der Mosel there's a legendary black cat the locals often talk about and referred to as "The Zeller Schwarze Katz". She's on the label of most of the wines that this region produces, and she has her own statue and fountain in the town square.

SO THE STORY GOES OF "THE ZELLER SCHWARZE KATZ"

"In 1863 there were 3 wine merchants from Aachen and they came into a wine cellar in Zell-Mosel to purchase the best wine they could find. In one winery, the negotiations went on for a long time and suddenly the cellar owner's black cat sprung up onto one cask. She arched her back threateningly and she hissed when these merchants came near her. The merchants interpreted this as a good omen [that a cat would defend a wine from price discounting] and they bought without even tasting the wine. Back in Aachen, the wine sold well [it was branded with a black cat on the label] and the merchants came back for more".

The Zeller region is famous for its high-quality Riesling. The collective and independent vineyards cover an area of 627 hectares and is thus one of the largest viticulture communities on the Mosel each producing their own version of "Zeller Schwarze Katz" wine, which have become known throughout the world.

Weingut H. J. & E. Lehmen Estates produces their version of "Zeller Schwarze Katz" Riesling, as well as other white wine varieties such as Kerner, Rivaner, Secco and Winzer Sekt; and Dornfelder, which is a typical German Red wine. The Rieslings are harvested between October and November, and are traditionally harvested by hand to guarantee premium quality. The wines are all cold fermented in stainless steel tanks, receiving daily checks to ensure quality. Although this is a more prolonged type of fermentation process, it is gentler on the wine.

Weingut Lehmen chooses to produce their wines using a balance of traditional wine making with modern techniques, which have produced award-winning brands. The Lehmen Estate wines have received numerous gold and silver medals from the German Chamber of Agriculture over the past few decades and most recently from the Beverage Tasting Institute (BTI) and Wine Enthusiast for its Rieslings.

The Winery also operates a bed and breakfast (Pension Haus "Edeltraud") hosted by Herman's wife, Edeltraud Lehmen. The Lehmen Guest House caters to wine lovers and wine "newbies" who love German wine and stay to experience the beauty of the countryside that Zell (Mosel) has to offer. Guests are always welcome to join in professional wine "tastings" and tours of the winery and vineyards the Lehmen Family offers.

Lehmen Estates has developed a loyal following who return to the winery each year.

Together, the Lehmen family continues to carry on the tradition into the next generation.

2010
Kerner
2010
Lehmen's
Trocken

Collesi

PROFILE OF AN ITALIAN CRAFT BREWERY

Birra Artigianale Collesi, referred to as Collesi, is a story about passion and excellence in the hand crafted beer market. Collesi represents a small family owned artisanal company, yet Tenute Collesi has achieved a leading position among small breweries both in Italy and abroad with the reputation for providing superior quality ingredients with the adherence to the procedures of old beer masters.

The beers are brewed at La Fabbrica Della Birra *(The Beer Factory)*, Tenute Collesi. The factory is located in the medieval village called Apecchio, at the border between Tuscany, Marche, Umbria and Romagna.

The factory is situated at 700 mts above sea level in the mountainous area of Monte Nerone. This strategic geographic location allows Collesi to exploit the pure and limpid natural spring water from Monte Nerone, which has the ideal characteristics for the beer production.

The brewery Tenute Collesi is located in the Apennine medieval village called Apecchio, next to Urbino, hometown to Raphael the painter, in a fantastically preserved and unpolluted mountainous area.

TENUTE COLLESI
BIRRA ARTIGIANALE
IMPERALE
Fiat lux
AMBRATA
COLLESI
TENUTE COLLESI
BIRRA ARTIGIANALE
IMPERALE
Ubi
ROSSA
COLLESI
TENUTE COLLESI
BIRRA ARTIGIANALE
IMPERALE
Maior
NERA
COLLESI
TENUTE COLLESI
BIRRA ARTIGIANALE
IMPERALE
Non Plus Ultra
LIMITED EDITION

Collesi

PROFILE OF AN ITALIAN CRAFT BREWERY

All of the Collesi beers are unpasteurized, unfiltered and naturally re-fermented in the bottle. They are brewed in small batches with traditional top fermenting methods, in order to preserve the quality of the selected raw materials to achieve full flavored beers, while keeping freshness, smoothness and pleasantness, blended in an elegant perlage.

Our philosophy is simple; we feel that excellence in brewing is all about finding the perfect balance between craft and science, between natural ingredients and processes.

The aroma of a Collesi beer is just the beginning of a long pleasure made of slow sips. It's a unique experience, because it's different from all other beers, thanks to our unique recipe, the ingredients, the long brewing process and the Italian artisanal craftsmanship.

This is a beer for any cuisine. Collesi beers make ideal pairings for all diverse flavors from around the world. It's a superior alternative to traditional beers for a discerning clientele and for special occasions.

WE PRODUCE A RANGE OF AWARD WINNING BEERS

AMBRATA

Amber Ale beer with a clean and intense aroma. This is an all-around beer that goes perfectly with any food that isn't sweet like pork or beef, grilled meat, BBQ, or Mexican.

BIONDA

Ale beer that shows a very fine gain, with a rich and creamy foam. Perfect for pasta, spicy sauces, fish and seafood.

CHIARA

Ale beer has an elegant and fruity flavor with intense aromas of malt and citrus fruits. A good thirst quencher that pairs well with appetizers, or light starters.

NERA

Stout beer with a full bodied taste, with a complex aroma of roasted coffee, barley, cocoa, liquorice and rhubarb. Great with dark chocolate or with many desserts with caramel and dried fruit.

ROSSA

Red Ale beer with a great personality offering a sweet with intense and spicy aroma of caramel, malt, hazelnuts. Great with desserts or as an after dinner drink.

We at Collesi control the entire production cycle, from raw materials to bottling. The barley comes from the farm belonging to the Collesi family, the malting is made in a modern malt house partially owned by Tenute Collesi, the water comes from the natural spring of Monte Nerone, the fermentation is totally made at La Fabbrica della Birra under the supervision of a Belgian beer master. The bottling and labeling are also handled at the factory.

Our family tradition in making beer is driven by our passion for excellence. For those seeking an alternative to wine, or a compliment pairing, our range of award-winning products truly pair "perfectly" with any of the recipes from appetizers to desserts.

1870
COLLESI

Medal Winners & Rated Labels

S Collesi Birra Imperala Bionda, Belgium style Italian craft beer, Apecchio, Italy. *Silver Medal at 2010 World Beer Championship*

B Aromo Viogner vintage 2010 from Maule Valley, Chile. *Vintage 2010 Bronze Medal/81 pts., Beverage Tasting Institute*

D 3 Girls Chardonany from Lodi, CA. *Vintage 2008 Double Medal at the Lodi Intn'l Wine Awards*

B Collesi Birra Imperale, family of Belgium style Italian craft beers, Imperala Chiara, Rossa and Nera, *Bronze Medals at NY Intn'l Beer Competition*

B Aromo Chardonnay from Maule Valley, Chile. *Vintage 2010 Bronze Medal/83 pts., Wine Enthusiast*

B Mo-Velt Grüner Veltliner from Austria. *Vintage 2010 Bronze Medal, 84 pts., Beverage Tasting Institute*

R Spaghetti Red (blend) from California's North Coast Region, *"Best Buy" 85 pts., Wine Enthusiast*

R Arona Sauvignon Blanc from Malborough, New Zealand. *Vintage 2009, 89 pts., Wine Enthusiast*

R Mutt Lynch's Unleashed Chardonnay. *Vintage 2009 88 pts., Anthony Dias Blue's The Tasting Panel*

R Weingut H.J. & E. Lehmen Estates, Zeller Schwarze Katz Riesling QbA, Hochgewächs Halbtrocken, *84 pts., Wine Enthusiast*

S Glory Days Zinfandel from Lodi, CA. *Vintage 2008 won Silver Medal/87 pts, Beverage Tasting Institute*

S Aromo Carménère from Maule Valley, Chile. *Vintage 2009 Silver Medal, 88 pts., Beverage Tasting Institute*

G Weingut H.J. & E. Lehmen, Kerner QbA, Mosel, Germany. *Gold Medal, 90 pts Wine Enthusiast*

G Esterházy Estoras Red from Burgenland, Austria. *Vintage 2009 won 92pts & was "Cellar Selection", Wine Enthusiast*

S St. Christopher Piesporter Goldtropfchen Kabinett from Mosel, Germany. *Vintage 2010 Silver Medal, 89 pts., Beverage Tasting Institute*

S Bauer Haus Auslese from Rheinhessen, Germany. *Vintage 2009 Silver Medal, 87 pts., Beverage Tasting Institute*

B Bauer Haus Sweet Red from Rheinhessen, Germany. *Vintage 2010 Bronze Medal, 82 pts., Beverage Tasting Institute*

G Weingut H.J. & E. Lehmen Estates, Zeller Schwarze Katz Riesling QbA, Hochgewächs Fruchtsüss. *Gold Medal BTI, 90 pts, and previous vintage, 86 pts Wine Enthusiast*

R Gelisi Antonio Moscato Dolce. *Rated "Exceptional Best Buy" Beverage Tasting Institute*

We have highlighted a list of the "Medal" winners and "Rated" labels that appear throughout the book on this chart.
*Please refer to the **Pairing Locator Guide** on page 236 for a comprehensive list of all the recommended labels specified on the recipe pages.*

17 58
ESTERHÁZY

AUSTRIA
ESTORAS

AROMO.
ESTATE BOTTLED
CARMÉNÈRE
D.O. MAULE VALLEY
PRODUCT OF CHILE · WINE OF CHILE
2009

BAUER HAUS AUSLESE
2009 RHEINHESSEN
PRÄDIKATSWEIN
WHITE WINE

ARONA
MARLBOROUGH
SAUVIGNON BLANC
2010
NEW ZEALAND

Spaghetti Red
CALIFORNIA
RED TABLE WINE

AROMO.
ESTATE BOTTLED
Viognier
D.O. MAULE VALLEY
PRODUCT OF CHILE · WINE OF CHILE
2009

CHARDONNAY
unleashed
CENTRAL COAST 2009

by MUTT LYNCH WINERY

BEER
FROM ITALY
IMPER ALE
Rossa
NET CONTENT 1 PINT, 9.36 FLUID OUNCES
COLLESI

WEINGUT-PENSION H.J.&E. LEHMEN
D-56856 ZELL-KAIMT/MOSEL
2010
RIESLING-
HOCHGEWÄCHS
HALBTROCKEN
ZELLER SCHWARZE KATZ
750 ml
MOSEL

AROMO.
ESTATE BOTTLED
CHARDONNAY
D.O. MAULE VALLEY
PRODUCT OF CHILE · WINE OF CHILE
2009

3 Girls
Chardonnay
ST. CHRISTOPHER
Piesporter Goldtröpfchen
Riesling Kabinett
Mosel

Villa Cattaneo · San Quirino
Gelosi Antonio
OLTREPO PAVESE
DENOMINAZIONE DI ORIGINE CONTROLLATA
MOSCATO DOLCE
VFQPRD DOLCE WHITE WINE

MO-VELT
GRÜNER VELTLINER

Weingut - Pension H.J. Lehmen
D-56856 Zell-Kaimt/Mosel · Tel: 0 65 42 / 46-28

www.lehmenwein.de
2008
Kerner
Qualitätswein

BEER
FROM ITALY
IMPER ALE
Bionda
NET CONTENT 1 PINT, 9.36 FLUID OUNCES
BAUER HAUS SWEET RED
2010 RHEINHESSEN
DEUTSCHER QUALITÄTSWEIN
SWEET RED WINE

Pairing Locator Guide

ORGANIZED BY FOOD GROUP & RECIPE PAGE NUMBER

Appetizers

Soups

Salads

Sides

Pastas & Sauces

*If you are unfamiliar with these label names, we have organized the **Pairing Locator Guide** by food group and recipe page number to help you locate each recommendation within the book. "Medal" winners and "Rated" labels are featured in bold.*

Main Dishes

Desserts

9

Reference Guide

PESTO
DIPPING & DRIZZLING OIL
OLIVIER
Napa Valley
BASIL, GARLIC, AGED PARMESAN AND LEMON
7.6 FL. OZ. (225ml)
BALSAMIC
10 years
MEDI TERRANEA
AGRUMATO
EXTRA VIRGIN OLIVE OIL PRESSED WITH ORANGES
7.04 fl. oz. (200ml)
OLIVIER
7.6 FL. OZ. (225ml)
CIDER APPLES
AB 0
CD 1
EF 2
GH 3
IJ 4
KL 5
MN 6
OPQ 7
RST 8
UVW
XYZ
CE

Weights, Measurements & Conversions

Pinch, Dash, and Smidgen are a lot like Bunch, Few, and Some—this is an approximate equivalent to old family recipes as best as we can tell. A pinch is what you can pick up between your fingers and thumb. But, for those that must know precisely, here are commonly accepted conversions you can use when interpreting your own family recipes.

FAMILY RECIPE MEASUREMENTS

MEASUREMENT	EQUIVALENTS
a Hint	tiny amount (½ drop)
a Drop	1/64 teaspoon (½ smidgen)
a Smidgen	1/32 teaspoon (½ pinch)
a Pinch	1/16 teaspoon (½ dash)
a Dash	⅛ teaspoon (½ tad)
a Tad	¼ teaspoon
1/4 stick butter	2 tablespoons
juice of a lemon	3 tablespoons
juice of an orange	½ cup

COOKING MEASUREMENT EQUIVALENTS

	tsp.	tbsp.	fl. oz.	cup	pint	quart	gallon
tsp.	1	⅓	⅙	1/48			
tbsp.	3	1	½	1/16	1/32		
oz.	6	2	1	⅛	1/16		
cup	48	16	8	1	½	¼	1/16
pint	96	32	16	2	1	½	⅛
quart	192	64	32	4	2	1	¼
gallon	768	256	128	16	8	4	1

Weights, Measurements & Conversions

U.S. TO METRIC MEASUREMENT EQUIVALENTS

CAPACITY

⅕ teaspoon	1 ml
1 teaspoon	5 ml
1 tablespoon	15 ml
1 fluid ounce (oz.)	30 ml
⅕ cup	50 ml
1 cup	240 ml
2 cups (1 pint)	470 ml
4 cups (1 quart)	0.95 liter
4 quarts (1 gal.)	3.8 liters

LIQUID

1 dash	6 drops
1 teaspoon	⅓ tbsp., 4.93 ml
1 tablespoon	1/16 cup, ½ fluid oz., 3 tsps., 14.79 ml
1 fluid ounce (oz.)	1/16 pint, 29.57 ml
1 cup	8 fluid oz., 16 tbsps, 237 ml
1 pint	2 cups, 473 ml
1 fifth	757 ml
1 quart	2 pints, 946 ml
1 gallon	4 quarts, 3.78 l

OZ.	LB.
1	1/16
2	⅛
4	¼
5	⅓
8	½
11	⅔
12	¾
16	1
32	20

WEIGHT

1 oz.	28 grams
1 lb.	540 grams

DRY

pinch	≈ ⅛ tsp.
1 ounce	1/16 lb., 28.35 g
1 peck	8 qts, ¼ bushel
1 pound	16 oz., 453.6 g

ABBREVIATIONS

cup	C.
ounce	oz.
quart	qt.
gallon	gal.
pint	pt.
pound	lb.
tablespoon	T. or tbsp.
teaspoon	t. or tsp.

Refrigerator, Freezer & Cooking Tips

Follow these simple tips to help store and cook foods safely.

- Purchase products *prior* to the "sell-by" or expiration date.
- Refrigerated foods should be stored at (40° F) to prevent foods from spoiling or becoming dangerous.
- Always follow handling recommendations on the package.
- Keep meat and poultry in its original package just before using.
- If freezing meat and poultry in its original package longer than 2 months, overwrap these packages with airtight heavy-duty foil, plastic wrap, freezer paper, or place the package in a plastic bag.
- Freezing 0° F (-18 C) keeps food safe indefinitely but the length of stay in the freezer effects the quality level of the food.
- Cook foods to the required minimum cooking temperatures:

  165 F ≥ Poultry, poultry stuffing, and stuffed meat.

  158 F ≥ Ground Beef, fish, and seafood.

  150 F ≥ Pork and foods containing pork.

  145 F ≥ Shell eggs and foods containing shell eggs.

FREEZER LIFE SPAN

CATEGORY	MONTHS
Bacon and sausage	1–2
Casseroles	2–3
Egg whites/ egg substitutes	12
Frozen dinners	3–4
Gravy meat or poultry	2–3
Ham, hotdogs and lunchmeats	1–2
Meat, uncooked roast	4–12
Meat, uncooked steaks or chops	4–12
Meat, uncooked ground	2–3
Meat, cooked	2–3
Poultry, uncooked whole	12
Poultry, uncooked parts	9
Poultry, uncooked giblets	3–4
Poultry, cooked	4
Soups and stews	2–3
Wild game, uncooked	8–12

Index